~~Writ~~e Right From God

Tom Bird

Sojourn, Inc.

Copyright © 2001 by Thomas J. Bird

All rights reserved. No part of this work may be reproduced or transmitted in any form by any means, electronic or mechanical, including photocopying and recording, or by any information storage or retrieval system, except as may be expressly permitted by the 1976 Copyright Act or in writing by the publisher.

Requests for such permissions should be addressed to:
Sojourn, Inc.
P. O. Box 4306
Sedona, Arizona 86336
www.Sojourninc.com

Bird, Thomas J.
~~Write~~ Right From God

Cover: Graphics by Manjari
Layout: J. L. Saloff

ISBN: 0-9707258-1-7

First Edition

About The Author

Tom Bird has been hard at work proving, refining and teaching his revolutionary approach to writing for nearly a quarter-century, which is longer than the total collective time Gabriele Rico, Julia Cameron, Betty Edwards (*Drawing on the Right Side of Your Brain*), and Natalie Goldberg had put in before they wrote their best selling books on writing and drawing.

A publicist for the Pittsburgh Pirates during the seasons when the team last won a World Series, Tom's breakthrough insight led directly to the sale of his first book, *Willie Stargell* (Harper & Row, 1984), which he, at the age of 24, co-authored with recently deceased Hall of Fame big leaguer Willie Stargell.

Tom began presenting writing courses based on his revelation at the University of Pittsburgh in 1984. Immediately, word spread about his unique ability to release students' inner writer. The demand from those eager to benefit from his powerful techniques and principles has since led him to over 900 teaching appearances at over 90 different colleges and universities.

Some of the sites he has visited include such distinguished institutions of higher learning as: Duke University, The College of William and Mary, The University of Texas, Ohio State University, The University of Nebraska, New York State University, and Old Dominion University (a more defined list follows).

A prolific writer, as well as teacher, Tom has penned nine additional books since the publication of Willie Stargell, and his byline has appeared in dozens of publications. Subsequent books include *KnuckleBALLs* (Freundlich Books, 1986), co-authored with big league Hall of Famer Phil Niekro; *Hawk* (Zondervan, 1996), written with future Hall of Famer Andre Dawson; *POWs of WWII: Forgotten Men Tell Their Stories* (Praeger, 1990); *Fifty-Two Weeks or Less to the Completion of Your First Book* (Sojourn, 1990); and *Literary Law* (Sojourn, 1986) (list follows). He has also contributed to such distinguished magazines and newspapers as *Parade, USA Today, The American Banker, The Pittsburgh Post Gazette* and *Sail* (list follows). Recently, he recreated the experience of his revolutionary workshops in an interactive computer program for writers, *The Author's Den*.

Tom's continued success as a writer has led his work to be featured in *USA Today*, the *New York Times*, the *Los Angeles Times*, the *Philadelphia Inquirer*, the *Chicago Sun-Times* and over 100 other publications (list of publications follows). His writing has also been featured on most of the top nation's news and interview programs including the *David Letterman Show, The Tonight Show, CBS Morning News, The Today Show, The Charlie Rose Show, CBC*, and the *700 Club* (list follows).

A year and a half ago, Tom founded Ambassador University, a long distance writing school, from which he offers his Intensive Writing Program (IWP), which leads his students to the completion of his or her first two books in record time.

Books and Software by the Author

Willie Stargell with Willie Stargell (Harper & Row, 1984)

How To Get Published (Sojourn, 1986)

KnuckleBALLs, with Phil Niekro (Freundlich Books, 1986)

Literary Law (Sojourn, 1986)

Beyond Words (Sojourn, 1987)

POWs of WWII: Forgotten Men Tell Their Stories (Praeger, 1990)

Fifty-Two Weeks or Less to the Completion of Your First Book (Sojourn, 1990)

The Author's Den interactive computer program (Sojourn, 1993)

Hawk, with Andre Dawson (Zondervan, 1994)

Hawk, the children's version (Zondervan, 1995)

Getting Published Now! (Sojourn, 2001)

Tom Bird"s Selective Guide to Literary Agents (Sojourn)

Publications Where the Author has Appeared

A prolific writer, as well as teacher of writing, Bird's own work has appeared in dozens of notable journals including:

Parade
USA Today
Popular Mechanics
New Writer's Magazine
Vegetarian Times
The American Banker
Racquetball Illustrated
Racquetball Everyone
Racquetball
Strength and Health Magazine
The Pittsburgh Post Gazette
Pittsburgh Magazine
Cleveland Magazine
Nautilus Magazine
Austin Magazine
Baseball America
Sail
Steeler Weekly
Erie Magazine
Erie Times News

Venues Where Author has Presented His Ideas

Tom Bird has shared his vision with tens of thousands of writers during more than 700 speaking appearances at 80+ at colleges, universities, and workshops from coast to coast and border to border, including:

Duke University
College of William and Mary
University of Texas
Florida Atlantic University
Temple University
University of Tennessee
Ohio State University
University of Nebraska
University of New Mexico
Penn State University
University of Arizona
University of Missouri
University of North Carolina
Memphis State University
Nova University
University of Florida
University of Cincinnati
University of Pittsburgh
Florida State University
Emory University
New York State University
University of Nevada - Las Vegas
Northern Arizona University
Florida International University
University of New Mexico
Louisiana State University
University of North Florida
Slippery Rock State University
Augusta State University
Central Florida University
University of Central Florida
Queens College
Robert Morris College
Mercyhurst College
Santa Fe Community College
Chautauqua Institute
Scottsdale Community College
Seton Hall College
Butler County Community College
Allegheny County Com. College
John Tyler Community College
J. Sargent Reynolds Com. College
Paul D. Camp Community College
Com. College of Cuyahoga County
Lakeland Community College
Beaver Valley Community College
Pima County Community College
Tidewater Community College
Colin County Community College
Mesa Community College
Paradise Valley Community College
Yavapai Community College
St. Petersburg Community College
Youngstown State University
Valdosta State University
Niagara University
Edinboro University
Indiana State University
Old Dominion University

Television and Radio Appearances

Mr. Bird is familiar to radio and television audiences due to dynamic presentations on his work and appearances on such high-profile national television and radio shows as the *David Letterman Show*, *The Tonight Show*, *CBS Morning News*, *The Today Show*, *The Charlie Rose Show*, *CBC*, and the *700 Club*. Highlights include:

Radio:

WBVP – Beaver, PA
WBUT – Butler, PA
WDAD – Indiana, PA
WDSY – Pittsburgh, PA
WJET – Erie, PA
WGLU – Johnstown, PA
WLTJ – Pittsburgh, PA
WORD – Pittsburgh, PA
WPIT – Pittsburgh, PA
WQED – Pittsburgh, PA
WQLN – Erie, PA
WTAE – Pittsburgh, PA
WWSW – Pittsburgh, PA
WHRO – Norfolk, Va
WTAE – Pittsburgh, PA
KDKA – Pittsburgh, PA
WGN – Chicago
WOR – New York
KQV – Pittsburgh, PA
WBCN – Boston
WSBR – Boca Raton
WJMK – Chicago
WBZ – Boston
WODS – Boston
KNBR – San Francisco
KGO – San Francisco
WFVD – New York
KMOX – St. Louis
KOST – Los Angeles
Moody Press Line – Chicago
WHYY – Philadelphia
WAXY – Miami
KEX – Portland, OR

Television:

David Letterman Show
The Tonight Show/Johnny Carson
The Today Show
CBS Morning News
Pittsburgh Today
Cleveland Today
The Charlie Rose Show
CBC
The 700 Club
WGN - Chicago
WTAE – Pittsburgh
KDKA – Pittsburgh
WOOR – New York
WMC – Memphis
WCFC – Chicago
WPIX – New York
WHDH – Boston
KMOX – St. Louis
KRON – San Francisco
WAVY – Norfolk
WPGH – Pittsburgh
WPXI – Pittsburgh
WEWS – Cleveland
KTVU – Oakland
WSVN – Miami
WHDH – Boston
WICU – Erie, PA
WJET – Erie, PA
WSEE – Erie, PA

To learn more about Tom's
Intensive Writer's Program (IWP),
or to receive information on when
or where he will be appearing,
feel free to check out his web site at
http://www.ambassu.com or
call his office at 928/203-0265.

Acknowledgements

Many hearts, souls and minds contributed to the successful completion and publication of this extraordinary book. Thank you to Jeremy Tarcher for his time and timely suggestions and insights; Jean Marie Stine for her editorial assistance, guidance and all around understanding and encouragement; Jamie Saloff for her refinement and formatting of my material; Elizabeth Richtor, Tom Puetz and Stephanie Patterson for their encouragement; Manjari for the cover; to my many students and their longings for this book; and most of all, to God, for the way, the reason, the time, the energy, the resources, the message, and the way.

Table of Contents

About The Author iii
    Books by the Author v
    Publications Where the Author has Appeared vi
    Venues Where Author has Presented His Ideas vii
    Radio: viii
    Television: viii
    Television and Radio Appearances viii
    Dedication: xv
How to Use This Book 01
Introduction 03
Chapter One: My Story 07
Chapter Two: Those Who Have Connected and Released 17
    The Creative Intellectual: Diana Theodores 17
    The Overworked Executive:Karen Stone 20
    The Busy Housewife: Patti Henry 22
    He Just Couldn't Get It Together: Tom Puetz 26
    She Had Always Wanted To Do This But Just Didn't Know
        How: Kristine Larson 26
**Chapter Three: Your Author Within and How Releasing It
    Will Change Your Life** 29
    The Essential Connection 30
    Have any of the following ever happened to you? 30
    Others Who Have Experienced It 31
    Common Characteristics of This Connected State While
        Writing 32
    What Is It? 33
    Coined as an Entity 34
    It is Your Essential Inspiration and Guide 36
    Meeting Your Author Within 37
**Chapter Four: What Caused Your AW To Go Into Hiding All
    Of These Years?** 41
    It All Begins with Society Who Tries to Sever Your
        Connection with Your AW 42
    Parents and Others 43
    How the Educational System Further Severs Our AW
        Connection 43
    Creating Self-Critism That Worries Over Minutia 44
    Misconceptions and BS 44
Chapter Five: Fears 47
    Fear of Success 47
    Examples of Fears of Success 48
    Fears of Change 48

Table of Contents

Fears of Loss 49
Examples of Fears of Failure 50
Fears of Lack 50
The Man or Woman in the Mirror:
The Good News is that You Can Reverse It 51
Five Statements 52
Chapter Six: The Eighteen CBs 53
The Logical / Critical Mind 55
Chapter Seven: The Three R's of Writing 59
Connection Breakers #1-3 61
Connection Breaker Number One: 61
These CBs sever your necessary connection with your AW ...61
Connection Breaker Number Two: 62
Connection Breaker Number Three: 63
The Three R's of Writing 64
Once The Three R's of Writing are employed: 65
'R' Number One: 66
The Three R's of Writing stand for: 66
'R' Number Two: 67
'R' Number Three: 68
The Semi-Round Room and the Elevator Ride to the Top ...69
**Chapter Eight: How Your AW Speaks to You or Through
You and, if You're a Writer, to Your Readers** 73
Understanding Your Archetypes 74
The Two Types of Archetypes 75
Transformational Archetypes 75
Common Characteristics of the Transformational Archetype .75
Primary Archetypes 77
Your Primary Archetypes Will Do the Writing for You 81
How Your PAs Will Introduce Themselves 84
Understanding the Backgrounds of Your PAs 85
Who Really are Your PAs? 88
PA in Non-Fiction 90
A Look Back and a Leap Forward 92
Chapter Nine: Let the Cards Do the Trick 97
What Are "The Cards" and Why Do They Work? 99
How We Will Use the Cards and What They Will Do for Us .101
Phase One – The Cathartic Cleansing 102
Testimonial 103
Sharon Newman: Week One of Working with Her Cards ...103
Sharon Newman: Week Two 104
Phase Two – Hello PA's 106

Table of Contents

Testimonial 107
Angelyn Bales: What it Felt Like to Work on the Index Cards
    During the First Few Weeks 107
Phase Three – The Living Outline 111
Beyond Phase Three 111
The CBs That #4, 5, 6 and 7 Disproves 112
Connection Breaker Number Four: 112
Connection Breaker Number Five: 113
Connection Breaker Number Six: 115
Connection Breaker Number Seven: 116
Putting "The Cards" into Play 117

Chapter Ten: Consistently Reinforce Your AW Dreams and What It Releases Through You 121
The Simple Truth 122
It Only Recognizes Associations with Pain and Pleasure . . . 125
The Two Steps 126
I "Chooses" 126
He Gained Twelve Pounds 127
You Can Gain Too 129
Negatory Stuff 130

Chapter Eleven: Reading 131
Connection Breaker Number Eight: 134
Cathartic Stage 135

Chapter Twelve: Commitment 137
The Contract 138
Before the Contract 141
Your Written Commitment to Living Your Dream 142
General Statement of Purpose 143
The Wager 147
Before Moving On 149
What Does This All Have to do With Connection Breaker
    Number Nine? 149

Chapter Thirteen: The Wider the Space, the More Passionate the Expression, the Better the Writing 157
What the AW Craves 158
Why This Works 159
But I Can't Read my Writing When I Write in Longhand . . . 160
But I Type so Much Faster and Write so Much Better
    at the Keyboard 161
Lineless Alternatives 162
Connection Breaker Number Ten: 163
Your Assignment 163

Table of Contents

Chapter Fourteen: Essential Suggestions to Live By 165
    Connection Breaker Number Eleven: 166
    I Am Thankfuls 166
    No Edit, No Read, Just Write 167
    Connection Breaker Number Twelve: 167
    I Wish 167
    Gaps 168
    Connection Breaker Number Thirteen: 168
    Keep the Flow Going by Ending in the Middle and Warming
      Up Before Resuming 168
    Connection Breaker Number Fourteen: 169
    Just Let the Words Fly 169
    Connection Breaker Number Fifteen: 169
    Writing as Fast as You Can 169
    Your Maximum Present Writing Speed 172
    How to Direct Your Maximum Speed With Your Writing 173
    Connection Breaker Number Sixteen: 175

Chapter Fifteen: Allowing Your AW to Write Your Project for You 177
    Connection Breaker Number Seventeen: 177
    A Few Last Minute Reminders 180
    Let's Go! 181

Chapter Sixteen: Enhancing **183**
    Connection Breaker Number Eighteen: 183
    The First Sweep Through 184
    After You Have Completed the Above 185
    Post Writing Research 185
    The Colors of the Rainbow 187
    The Pianist in Us All 189
    Let Your Computer Go to Work for You 189
    One Final Read Through 190
    Publication 191
    Testimonial 191
    Rosemary O'Keeffe on the submission of her query letter ...191
    Where to Go Now 194

Dedication:

I dedicate this book to my close and dear friend Willie 'Pop' Stargell who unselfishly and lovingly shared with me all I would ever need to know.

Our deepest fear is not that we are inadequate.
Our deepest fear is that we are
Powerful beyond measure.
It is our Light, not our
Darkness, that most frightens us.
We ask ourselves, Who am I to be brilliant,
Gorgeous, talented, fabulous?
Actually, who are you not to be?
You are a child of God.
Your playing small does not serve the World.
There is nothing enlightening about
Shrinking so that other people
Won't feel unsure around you.
We were born to make manifest the
Glory of God that is within us.
It is not just in some of us; it is in everyone.
As we let our own Light shine,
We unconsciously give other people
Permission to do the same.
As we are liberated from our own fear,
Our presence automatically
Liberates others.

Nelson Mandela, Inaugural Speech, 1994

How to Use This Book

Whether you are a seeker of the ultimate connection, an author, or an aspiring writer, or all three, this book has been designed specifically for you.

Unlike other inspirational, self help books though that suggest you first read through the text, then come back and do whatever exercises you skipped over on your initial run through, I do not encourage that. The exercises in this book are simply way too important. Were you to skip them and the massive amount of understanding that they offer, you would be cutting yourself off from much of what this book can share with you.

In fact, each of the exercises in which you will be asked to participate are so important, that it is essential that you familiarize yourself with the following foundational steps before you begin employing them.

Simply take time to read over the following and then do so again as you come upon the enlightening experience that you chose to receive by choosing this book in the first place.

Here they are:

- First, make sure to find yourself each and every time before beginning an exercise in a quiet, comfortable space in which you will be uninterrupted.

- Second, make sure that you have a pen and some lineless paper sitting in front of you.
- Third, before entering into this exercise, make sure that your arms and legs remained uncrossed, and hanging free at all times.
- Fourth, do all your breathing in and out through your nose only.
- Fifth, when beginning the exercise, close your eyes and keep them closed until you are ready to write.
- Sixth, if at any time you feel tense, for any reason at all, breathe in deeply through your nose and then blow out all of your tension through your mouth, before going back to both inhaling and exhaling through your nose only.
- Seventh, if at any time during this writing experience you feel as if you have run out of something to say or the speed of your writing has dropped drastically, close your eyes, breath out any tension and reconnect with the image that caused you to write in the first place.
- Eighth, write as fast as you can at all times, not taking any time to edit or read over your work ever.
- Ninth, write how ever the words come out onto the paper. Don't worry about columns or any other special arrangements. Just let your words go where they want and project themselves how ever they want.
- Last, to make it easier for yourself, you may choose to employ the use of a tape player to record in advance and then play back for yourself the steps that follow for each of the exercises.

Have fun,

Tom

Introduction

"I know God will not give me anything I can't handle. I just wish that He didn't trust me so much." Mother Teresa

I began writing this book for authors and aspiring writers. However, the further I got into the writing, the more the book took off on its own direction. Soon, I realized that I was no longer just writing a book about writing. Instead I was writing about making the connection we all seek with our Almighty, Higher Power, Right Brain, Heart, Greater Consciousness, Source, or whatever you choose to call He, She, or It.

As reluctant and as unqualified as I felt, I allowed the book to go where it was that it wanted to go.

Within the pages of this book I will share with you how the writing of that long-awaited book or screenplay, in 90 days or less, will serve as the catalyst to making the direct connection we all seek.

Part 1:

We Already Have What We Need

"Believe nothing, no matter where you read it, or who said it – even if I have said it – unless it agrees with your own reason and your own common sense."
- Buddha

Chapter One: My Story

"Why do they call them tellers? They never tell you anything. They just ask questions. And why do they call it interest? It's boring. And another thing - how come the Trust Department has all their pens chained to the table?"
Coach Ernie Pantusso, "Cheers"

At the age of fourteen, as I laid on my parents' side lawn staring up at the stars, I asked a question of that which I had been connected to as a child, a query that had been burning inside of me for years.

"Why is it that I want to write?"

Even though we all have the capacity to see, hear and feel, some people receive internal communication best audibly, while others rely on visual. Me, I'm primarily kinesthetic. I *feel* the result of my communications. And since I have been tuned into that form of communication since I was a very young child, it is as natural and as effective for me, if not more so, than hearing a voice on high.

After asking my question that evening, I could feel the unmistakable intention of the reply pulsating through every fiber of my body. And IT said, *"You want to write because that is your way of conveying all that you see in a manner that maybe others will begin to see, and thus benefit by that which can come so naturally to all."*

An obsession from my childhood began to make sense immediately afterwards. It all began just after I turned six years old. For Christmas that year, an aunt and uncle had given me a two foot by three foot cork bulletin board, which I hung in my room. Immediately after hanging it up, a never ending stream of words began pouring out of me. I began to copy them down on anything that was available and tacking them up on the board.

In no time at all, the corkboard was completely full. So I began using the tacks to hold more than one scrap of paper. Soon the tacks would hold no more. Shortly after, I began capturing my inspirations in notebooks; it was also at this time that I realized I was a writer.

That is how easy it came for me. In fact, I finished in the top two percentile nationally in communication skills on my college entrance exams, this after I had literally refused to participate in any form of studying in high school.

Another time in college, I deliberately got fall-down drunk before seeing a play I had been assigned to review. To make the school newspaper's tight deadline, I had only twenty-five minutes to complete my review after the completion of the play. I wrote the piece in less than fifteen minutes.

I had my date deliver the piece for me. I had received a significant number of compliments on my writing up to that point, but never as many as I received from that piece.

My theory about the naturalness of writing had once again been proven correct.

Shortly after graduating from college, I moved onto a one season, temporary position with big league baseball's Pittsburgh Pirates, and for the first time in my life I tried to become like everyone else. I had only taken the job because of my love for baseball, which was far secondary to how deeply I felt for writing. In fact, I had possibly been the only senior on campus that hadn't applied for any jobs. I didn't want a job. I wanted to write, to author. I hadn't ever been clearer on anything in my young life up to that point.

However, despite my academic complacency in high

"The first rule if you want to be a writer, is to be yourself."
Col. Henry Potter, M.A.S.H. #4077

"If I repent of anything, it is very likely to be my good behavior."
Thoreau

"Most people put off till tomorrow that which they should have done yesterday."
Edgar Watson Howe

school, I was an outstanding student. So the school, in an effort to further their reputation, fixed me up, sight unseen, in my position with the Pirates.

That year was 1979, the year of Willie "Pop" Stargell and the "Familee," the most charismatic group of ballplayers in the modern era of baseball. We won the World Series that season, in dramatic fashion, of course. Pop brought us back from a three-games-to-one deficit to win a deciding Game Seven with a classic homerun that he had promised to hit only a few hours before for an eleven-year boy dying of leukemia.

"I always say, keep a diary and someday it'll keep you."
Mae West.

I never had any aspirations of staying with the Pirates beyond that season. In fact, with the World Series I had always wanted to win as a kid under my belt, I was planning to follow my heart to New York, where I was going to settle in and write my first book. However, I had become a fixture with the Familee. So I was offered a big raise and a permanent position was established just for me; so I stayed.

But the writer in me kept calling to be let out. It relentlessly drove me to use whatever few free hours I had away from my job, to feverishly continue to follow the callings of my heart. By that time, practicality had set its roots in me. As a result, for the first time I thought I had to be an authority on writing and publishing to become the author I longed to be. I forgot all about the naturalness of the activity. I recognized that my collegiate education hadn't been able to offer me what I sought.

So I took to reading every book on writing that I could find over an eighteen-month span, filling one hundred and forty-eight legal pads with notes. In those pads I had hoped to find the magic formula that so many sought. However, once I reviewed my notes all I found was contradiction. Well thought of sources seemed to agree on nothing.

"If at first the idea is not absurd, then there is no hope for it."
Albert Einstein

I then turned to the biggest asset that I had going for me at that time: my job, which put me in the company of many a best-selling and worldly author. Liberally utilizing my extensive contacts, I began interviewing every author I could. To each I asked the same question, "*how do you become an author?*" The best answer I got was from Dick Young, the so-called

Dean of American Sports Writers at the time, who replied to my question by simply saying, *"you write."* I initially poo pooed Dick's response, not realizing its true significance.

I kept going because I did not believe that God would have given me such a strong calling to write without providing me with the route to live it; of that, I was sure. I was convinced I just had to find the necessary formula that so many hundreds of thousands, if not millions, had sought before me on not only how to easily and enjoyably write books, but get them published, as well. But it was nowhere to be found in all of the obvious places that I looked nor within all the orthodox methods that I considered.

By my fourth season with the Pirates and for the first time in my life, I had become a very unhappy young man. Initially, I blamed my inability to further my writing career as the reason.

Finally, out of desperation I got down on my knees and asked for Divine Guidance. I expressed my frustration. I shared the fears that I had about living my life without being able to live my dream, and how I felt that doing so was really dying. It was at that time that I realized the true reason for my despair. The reason that I was feeling as I did had to do with the fact that I had sold out my connection with God, which had come so naturally for me, and which had always been my most valuable asset, for the practicality of life.

It was also at that time, that I promised to share whatever it was that God would offer me with others in the same boat, so that they hopefully wouldn't have to suffer as long or as hard as I had been suffering.

Two mornings later I woke up hours before my alarm was set to go off, and I heard the words of Dick Young rolling around over and over again in my head. It was then that I finally realized I had started searching and stopped writing, which was the very reason my connection with God had been severed. And so, I began to do what had once come so naturally for me. In response, the words literally seemed to write themselves, with little or no effort from me. In fact, I felt stronger, jazzed, after writing the four thousand or so words that sprung from me that morning than I did

'Faith is the bird that feels the light and sings when the dawn is still dark."
Rabindranath Tagore

"Great men are they who see that spiritual is stronger than any material force and that thoughts rule the world."
Emerson

before I had begun. I could see a clearer and deeper meaning behind everything. I knew exactly what it was that I needed to do - which was to write - write and continue to write daily, every hour, every minute that I could squeeze out of my day. For embedded in the act of actually doing so, as most writers miss, is the faith, the wisdom, and the direction one needs to succeed.

I also clearly understood that I didn't have to try to be something that I already was. I had already connected back with what I eventually coined as my Author Within (AW), my true and absolute connection to the natural communicative abilities God has given everyone of us, that I had left behind when I tried to figure out how to become an author.

As a result of that realization, amazing things began happening in my life. Overnight my AW urged me to approach Willie, the most popular athlete in the country at the time, about co-authoring his life story. This was an intimidating assignment. For I knew that Willie had been severely taken advantage of by another writer a few years earlier. This author had chosen to fabricate certain aspects of Willie's story to make it a more sensational read. Since opting out of the deal, Willie had sworn never to become embroiled in a project like that one again. However, after working together through one World Series victory and the Pirates next three seasons, Willie and I had become very close friends. I was hesitant to approach him, though, since I didn't in any way want to endanger my friendship with him.

Nonetheless, the draw to speak with him wouldn't let me go. I finally approached him and confessed my aspirations, I candidly shared with him the reason behind my desire to speak with him. Willie listened attentively and compassionately, as he always did. He then shared his reflections of the pain, frustration, and embarrassment he, his friends and his family had suffered at the hands of his former co-author. Yet, he concluded by telling me that there was one and only one person that he would ever trust enough to ever enter into a venture of that sort with again...and I was that person.

"The only service a friend can really render is to keep up your courage by holding up to you a mirror in which you can see a noble image of yourself."
George Bernard Shaw

Man: Do you belong here?
Fonzie: I belong everywhere.
Happy Days

I began to see how my dream of becoming an author had never given up on me, even though I had tried to give up on it. It was willing to follow me wherever it was that I went, and patiently led me back around to where it was best for me to go.

Never having sold a book before, I once again asked for Divine Guidance. Shortly after arriving in my office later the following morning, the man who ran our mailroom came in with my morning's stack of mail. In that stack was a brochure from Scott Meredith, a literary agent in New York; how he had gotten my address I did not know. Nor did I know at the time that Scott was the top literary representative in the world.

So, unknowingly, I casually picked up the phone and gave his office a call. After I explained why I was phoning, his receptionist quickly paged me through to Scott's direct line. Once Scott heard what I had to say, he couldn't wait to meet with Willie and me. Coincidentally, the team was scheduled to be in Manhattan the following week to play the New York Mets, and a meeting was scheduled.

Once the three of us were together, an immediate kinship formed. Scott gave both Willie and me his private home phone number, signed us to a contract and we were on our way.

Six weeks later, Scott sold my first book to Harper & Row, the third largest publisher in the world, and Larry Ashmead, one of the business's finest editors. And, Scott sold it for an amount way beyond what I thought was possible, one equal to three times my yearly salary.

All of this transpired less than two months after I directly reconnected back with my Author Within. Since then, I have discovered via the people I have taught to connect with their own AW, that this kind of miraculous event is typical.

However, as wonderful as my sale was, I found myself faced with the daunting dilemma of having to write the book, and I had no idea how to go about doing so. But there was one thing that I had become very good at over the last few months, and that was reconnecting with and listening to my AW.

"Many of life's failures are people who did not realize how close they were to success when they gave up."
Thomas Edison

I was still working with the Pirates at the time, which meant that I was still responsible for working seven days a week and an average of fifteen hours a day. To accommodate my commitment to our publisher, I got up two hours early each morning to write. By following the daily directions of my AW, within six months I was able to complete a manuscript that brought Willie to tears, and which our editor praised as a strong, literary work.

It was my second book, though, that allowed me to perfect, and then be able to convey the specific steps and understandings about how to write a book.

"I will work in my own way, according to the light that is in me."
Lydia Maria Child

I was living in a bustling suburb of Pittsburgh at the time. Pittsburgh has a reputation for many things. But for those of us who have lived there, the traffic jams created by its many tunnels was one of the biggest. I make no bones about it, I despise traffic. I realize that no one likes it, but because I dislike traffic so much more than most, I am willing to do literally anything I can to avoid it. As bad as the traffic is in Pittsburgh during weekday rush hours, it was nearly as bad on the weekends when most people were off work.

So entering into my second book, I made the decision to test what I had learned by working only on the weekends, when the traffic in my neighborhood was usually at a standstill. My thinking was that not only would I be able to avoid the traffic I disliked so much, but I would also be able to evaluate what I thought I learned from my first book.

"The multitude of books is a great evil. There is no limit to this fever of writing."
Martin Luther

By then, I had come to theorize that the reason a person wanted to write had nothing to do with the actual act of writing itself. Instead this person sought to write because he or she had a book signed, sealed and delivered inside them that was dying and trying to get out. That which routinely stood in our ways of this natural, Divinely led act, I coined *Connection Breakers* (CBs).

My educated and tested belief in the perspective, that the books we long to write are already written inside of us, which had been illustrated by the results of many a famous writer, also led me to the theorize that if this were true then we should be able to relay these already finished works onto paper in about the same amount of time that it would take us literally to copy down that book. The more we limit the affects of CBs, the faster we would be able to write and the more clearer and perfected the draft of the work would appear.

With this theory in mind, I laid out the schedule to complete the writing of my second book. I figured that it would take twelve days of relaying words onto paper. Thus, if my theory on the perfection of the material released at such a high rate were actually valid and true, I would be able to review, revise, and perfect the entire draft of my 80,000 word manuscript in *three days or less*. Altogether, the time for the releasing and the revising added up to fifteen days or five three-day weekends.

> "God is love, but get it in writing."
> Gypsy Rose Lee

Much to my delight, creating the formal timeline calmed the concerns and fears of my AW's staunch adversary, my critical mind. As a result, I was able to give in to the process even more deeply and easily. Right from the beginning of the writing, I could tell that I was onto something major. The words began flowing out of me like water spraying out of a hose. Even more important was the fact that I loved the way I felt when I wrote. I looked forward to it so much that it became positively addictive.

I zoomed through the writing and revision of my second book, from first word to last in the five consecutive, three-day weekends I had allotted. To be on such a roll and to be able to reach that stage with my book in that short of an amount of time, was an unfathomable high. I was still reeling from the effects of my excitement as I slipped my manuscript into the mail to my publisher.

> "Don't play for safety – it's the most dangerous thing in the world." Hugh Walpole

However, stagnant time for a writer is the mother of all doubt. Sitting idle can cause a mountain of problems, as your critically-minded left brain, and all of its connection breakers, worries and fears finally catch back up with you, which is exactly what happened in my case. In a mere few days, my opinion of the experience had completely changed and I was more than sure I had just made the biggest mistake of my life.

Ten days after I had mailed in the manuscript, I

Tom Bird - ~~Write~~ Right From God

could no longer control myself. I had to call my publisher.

To my surprise he had not only loved the book, but had found so few mistakes that he didn't feel that any sort of rewriting was necessary.

So confident was I feeling with the methods that I had employed that I chose to employ the exact same methods to my third book, which I had been given five months to write. My publisher, Zondervan, was deeply concerned that the deadline was too tight, so they gave me a larger than average advance to compensate for my inconvenience.

I didn't want to disillusion them about how hard this would be to do, so even though I completed the book in a month and a half, I waited the remainder of the five months before I turned it in.

True to my word, soon afterwards I began following through on my promise to God to share with other aspiring writers that which I had learned. In no time, word spread through the local and then national writing communities of my work. Over the next eighteen years, I gleefully divided my time between the writing of my next nine books and making over 900 appearances at over 90 colleges and universities.

Then while standing in front of a packed classroom at the University of Arizona in January of 2000, I was overcome with the strangest of feelings. I recognized it as my own AW coming through.

By that time, I had learned the value of always following the advice of my Author Within, which on this occasion was nudging me to take those in attendance that day in a direction I had never steered anyone ever before. Shortly after, in listening to my AW, I upgraded my system to directly emulate that which I had offered that day.

Once implemented, I began seeing aspiring writers from all ages, beliefs, and backgrounds composing more than 10,000 words finished per day, and completing books and screenplays in as little as two or three weeks. In fact, the first fifty students to whom I chose to share this program, completed over 100 books with no compromises in quality.

What's the secret behind these amazing results?

"Creative activity could be described as a type of learning process where the teacher and the pupil are located in the same individual."
Arthur Koestler

"You can't build a reputation on what you're going to do."
Henry Ford

Reconnecting and then remaining connected with the Author Within. It will do the same for you, as this book will show.

Chapter Two:
Those Who Have Connected and Released

"Worth begets in base minds, envy; in great souls, emulation."
Henry Fielding, 1707-1754

One of the most challenging actions any of us would ever consider taking on would be the writing of a book. Yet, when connected in the right way, this and anything else, is well within your means, as the following sampling of testimonials, from persons with no proven prior experience with writing, illustrates.

The Creative Intellectual: Diana Theodores

"My professional writing life was triggered in the 60's through the world of dance. Doing, viewing, and writing about dance was my passion by the early age of fifteen, an adolescent aspiring to be a dance critic! My Dad said *'ring up the head honcho in the business*

Tom Bird - ~~Write~~ Right From God

> *"We should be taught not to wait for inspiration to start a thing. Action always generates inspiration. Inspiration seldom generates action."*
> Frank Tibolt

> *"You have no idea what a poor opinion I have of myself, and how little I deserve it."*
> W.S. Gilbert

(Clive Barnes at the New York Times then) *and get some advice.'* So, with my "Sunday best" of dance reviews tucked into a folder I knocked at Mr. Barnes' apartment door and held my breath. The all-powerful "make or break'em" critic of the NYT couldn't have been more gracious. He offered me a BLT sandwich, read my pieces, and said something like *'Well done...keep at it for ten more years and you'll be a dance critic...'* I was elated with the *'well done'* and despairing of the *'ten years'* which, to a fifteen year old (or anyone, come to think of it) seemed like a lifetime. I did, indeed *'keep at it'* and eventually published volumes of reviews and articles as dance critic for a national Sunday paper, and as a university academic. As a dance journalist I had experience with fast track deadlines, action writing (verbs on parade), vivid descriptive powers and a good memory. Academic or scholarly writing as part of my university career equipped me with research skills (thousands of 3x5 index cards bearing footnotes and annotations ritualistically burned at the end of each publication) and a begrudging yet dutiful practice of drafting and redrafting over and over in search of that *'original contribution to the field,'* etc.

"For the last five years I've been longing, hankering, yearning to write fiction. I have a lot of stories to tell and a voice that wants to be heard. If I could, I'd sing them - really belt them out - one outrageously eclectic aria after another. If you want to be heard you need fire in your belly and I have been searching for that heat for a long time. And this brings me to Tom Bird's IWP. Last year I declared a self-created sabbatical from my university post in England and came to New Mexico to re-ignite the fire (no, I didn't start the State burning) and to write to my heart's content (and write from my heart). I know. I sound like a walking cliché. The shock of freedom made me shy. I sat in my friend's sculpture studio (lovingly reorganized to accommodate my writing) day after day, typing journal entries, organizing notes from the archives of files I'd brought with me, and attempting some short stories (a collection of eight in first and second draft form). All the while a sensation sat in my gut. Now what are you waiting for? Write the novel. Let one story unfold and follow its course. I repeated to myself what I had heard from writing workshops, things about mastering the short story before moving on to the longer piece, or developing technique with language and structure through exercises before actually writing a story, and so on. Although I enjoyed working on my stories (and very much want to return to them) and the luxury of "playing" with writing every day, I knew that the one thing I really wanted to experience was the sustained focus of writing a novel. I also believed that writing is a physical act (coming from the dialogue I've had with writing and choreographing) and that I would need to acquire the physical stamina for the long haul of writing.

"Purely by chance I saw Tom's workshop advertised in the University of New Mexico special courses literature and enrolled. When this young man with hair flowing down past his shoulders walked into the seminar room I have to admit I sneered mentally. What does he think he's going to teach ME about writing? By the end of the session I was the first person to sign up to work with Tom on his intensive course, with one-to-one mentoring. What he had to say about writing as a physical act made sense. What he had to say about needing physical stamina and conditioning in order to maintain flow made sense. What he had to say about writing as releasing rather than constructing made sense. What he had to say about discipline made sense. And his optimistic attitude towards time made sense: Why not get as much done in as short a time as possible? What was a revelation for me was that all the items on my wish list (physical discipline, release, sustained focus, writing from the heart, finished product) were integrated here in one method of working and living.

"I wrote 194,000 words on large poster boards in five weeks and the experience has been exhilarating and provocative. Naturally, the main doubts and fears throughout, when they raised their heads, were about the literary merit of the writing, how, if or when the story would ever come to an ending, and how the hell I was going to type it all. The story did come to an end

"There is the risk you cannot afford to take, [and] there is the risk you cannot afford to take."
Peter Drucker

> "Far better it is to dare mighty things, to win glorious triumphs even though checkered by failure, than to rank with those poor spirits who neither enjoy nor suffer much because they live in the gray twilight that knows neither victory or defeat."
> Theodore Roosevelt

all on its own, as Tom assured me it would; the quality of the writing is yet to be assessed but I'm certain of the quality of the experience of the writing in any case. Tom's been much more than a writing facilitator. He's been a superb motivational coach and a spirit guide during this journey in my life. I have begun my second book and I feel like I have the energy and passion to write many more."

The Overworked Executive: Karen Stone

"There has always been a place inside me where words live. A place where the dark nights and the bright days of my life constantly parade themselves through my mind in a single line of affiliated letters. Sometimes the flow is too much for my mind to hold and through the years, these symbols flowed over into journals, 3X5 cards, post-it notes and old envelopes pulled from the side pocket of my purse at traffic lights. Sometimes words and phrases haunt me. The only way to get them to go away is to write them down. This has been going on from my earliest days. I Still have my diary from when I was 7 years old, and the vast array of miscellaneous notebooks and journals I have filled up over the years. I have always been connected to writing. I was editor of my elementary and junior high school newspapers. I got perfect marks on writing assignments all through school. As a teenager, I won a national essay contest for my area. I entered college intending to be a journalist or a newscaster or a dancer. Along with the gift of words I had, I had been given the gift of gab and movement. I chickened out when I heard the voice inside that said - you will never make very much money doing these things unless you are really, really good. I settled for what seemed like a more sure bet - the business world.

> "When we were little we had no difficulty sounding the way we felt; thus most little children speak and write with real voice."
> Peter Elbow
> Writing With Power

"I kept filling up notebooks, napkins and margins of meeting notes. My writing seeped into my corporate career. Outside of the parameters of my job descrip-

> "Give them great meals of beef and iron and steel, they will eat like wolves and fight like devils."
> Shakespeare

tions, I always seemed to be writing the important reports, presentations, and company brochures. I became known for my skill at editing memos on delicate subjects. There were hints all around me that kept throwing words and writing in my face. I dreamed of being a writer and several times began books on the most arousing emotional topic of the day for me - usually my relationships with men. One of the ultimate and most direct of compliments came in my late 30's when I was in graduate school. I was going through the first of several mid-life crises and decided to get a Masters in Social Work. On one of the margins of a term paper, one of my professors wrote, *'If social work should fail you, be a writer'*. But I was scared to try. I wanted to keep my dream of writing something significant and personal in front of me rather than really going for it. I was afraid of failing. I kept running away from it and into things that didn't matter that much. I used the excuses of money and time and nothing to say. And I kept filling up journals and shoeboxes with short sprints of inspiration.

"Several months ago, frustrated with my current professional engagement, I went to a one-day writing workshop. I just wanted to do something creative and to breakup the tension of my shaky career. I was exhausted that morning and almost did not get out of bed. I thank God everyday I did. That was the day I met Tom. I approached him at the first break and mumbled something about wanting to write articles. I live my life in sprints and short spurts of inspiration and energy. I had no intention of writing a book or running a marathon. He said to stay with the class and just see what happened. During the second half of the class, Tom took us through an exercise about what we wanted to write. A piece of a book I had been thinking about writing for over fifteen years started to fall out onto the poster board precariously balanced in front of me across the too small desk top. I thought of the box in my guest room closet that held my many attempts to do something with the emotions and ideas that came and went at odd times. Shortly thereafter, I started to work with Tom as an individual student in his Intensive Writer's Program. I began doing yoga

> "There is no security on this earth, there is only opportunity."
> General Douglas MacArthur

every morning and writing for several hours before going to the office. At night, I settled in and went for it again. I was able to walk between my Vice Presidential responsibilities during the day and the revealing of my deepest inner self through my writing in the mornings and at night. I have been on a conscious spiritual path for years and now those things that had become second nature to me became strongholds, supporting my creativity and allowing me to keep going through the emotional evolution that was happening. I talked to Tom everyday. I surrendered to his guidance and developed a deep trust of him as a man and a mentor. His voice was, and is, my lifeline to a new life. He has become the midwife of my soul, taking me through the throes of the birth of my personal transformation. For one month, I wrote whatever came to me and I filled board after board with words and segments of something that did not make much sense. In frustration one day, I asked Tom what to do. He took me through an exercise that broke something free inside of me and the book that had been hiding deep within started to pour out.

"Within four weeks, I had written over 120,000 words. I laughed, I cried. I fell asleep on the floor and on top of my boards. No matter what, I kept going. I finished on Easter morning. In the first light of sunrise, I sat in absolute amazement and gratitude, looking at the rough draft of the book I had always wanted to write. It had risen from the space inside of me that had been frozen solid until Tom came into my life. It is outside of me now for the first time. And I did all this in the few quiet hours before my workday started, at nights and on weekends."

The Busy Housewife: Patti Henry

"I have a box full of stories, poems and unfinished Novels from the age of twelve. Included in this box is my auto-biography (I assume I deemed my life worthy

> *"Courage is the price that life exacts for granting peace. The soul that knows it not, knows no release from little things; knows not the livid loneliness of fear, nor mountain heights where bitter joy can hear the sound of wings."*
> *Amelia Earhart*

of one at the time). After I received my first creative writing paper-back from the teacher, full of red marks, comments (faulty exposition) and intense grammatical errors, I put this box in a container with the paraphernalia of youth. I laid it with my yearbooks, diaries, old photos, ticket stubs and ribbons – labeled the container both emotionally and literally: *Nostalgic Things of the Past*. I then pursued things of greater logic and reality - Nursing.

"Opinion does not come into play in the matters of scientific fact. This I could do well, and correctly, getting my Master's in Pediatrics and publishing my thesis. See, I *published*. I would not let the fact that it was not *'The Book'* bother me. I was a published author. Time to move on. Through the years, my marriage and the birth of my three amazing children, this box and its writings would come to me in small nudgings, a minute passing of memory. I would look at it for what I had labeled it, regarded it with sweet memory and put it back in its proper location: the past. As the years went by its voice, its nudgings became louder, harder until I finally decided that the only way to shut it up was to just write the one book. Write the one good book and be done with it. How hard could that be? I started it. I threw it away. I read a book on writing novels, then I read another one. I got a writer's magazine and started again. I found my reasons, my excuses not to really write, but still pursue it. I read about it and researched it (that's what you do with all good disciplines). So, what now? A class, surely a class would be good. There was one by Tom Bird, for novice writers, on a Saturday that looked good. But, all day Saturday? I do have a family to take care of. I planned on going until boredom set in, and then leave early. At least I could say I went to a class on writing. I was vaguely pursuing my dreams, not totally caving in.

> *"Conformity is the jailer of freedom and the enemy of growth."*
> *John F. Kennedy*

"I sat in the very back - the seat you would never get called on in and escape out the back door was only three steps away. This man comes in the room; damn his hair was longer then mine. Great, a whole Saturday gone listening to some hippie tell me how to find my inner child and pull my creative powers from a universal source. I was glad I had made the wise

"The test of any man lies in action."
Pindar, 522-433 B.C.

choice to sit in the back: escape the clear alternative. Then he started talking. I wanted to run, sprint to the front row. More, more, more, give me more information. I didn't escape out the back, I mourned lunch hour (because we had to stop) and moved down a few rows (I still did not want to be called on). It all made so much sense; releasing the story (not creating), the physical act of writing, the fears of writing. He talked about writing being a call to communicate at some deep level, to leave something behind. He talked of writing and living from the heart, about not reaching the core of your feelings without writing. He gave practical steps (time, no distractions, relax, free writing). His steps to writing, moving to the right brain, gaining proper perspective and the symptoms of good writing all made sense. He touched on all of this and so much more, and for once in my life I had nothing to say. I was too busy listening (Those who know me don't believe this part).

"I went home and gushed to my husband *'I am finally going to do this, I really am.'* Well, I would prove it. I immediately wrote my contract (Step one) and began to e-mail and call Tom to try to get him to evaluate my query letter. During this time my fears had crept, woven their way back into my solid world. I had now decided I would take this slowly. Then I talked to Tom and found I had somehow agreed to do the IWP. I now stood with a commitment in hand and fear traveling my spine and gut in rippling nausea. I knew it was the right thing for me and I understood it was the only way to get it done with my fears, my husband, and my 7, 5 and 2 year old children all giving me excuses not to. We talked the next day to figure out a plan, a goal and a schedule. We talked for a long time about my days, how they were structured, what I did, my health, and my family. I did not see until later why all that was so important. I was just going to write, right? I have been doing it in journalistic and devotional form since I was ten years old. Just changing the pattern now couldn't have anything to do with my health. But, I went along with it until Tom said, *'OK, I've decided that the best thing for you is to get up and write from 4:30 - 6:30 am.'* I completely assumed he was joking and told him I only got up at that hour for babies and sick children. *'Not now,'* he told me, *'now you get up to write.'* Well, I had taken it this far; it was worth a shot. Tom warned me of the emotional and physical reactions I would have. I didn't believe him. Surely it was an exaggeration from a man whose life revolved around writing. Fatigue, from rising at an ungodly hour before the children, was the only symptom I expected (emotional or otherwise). So, I rose at 4:30am and wrote 3,000 words. Twice I dreamt I woke, wrote and called Tom, only to arise to the face of my 7-year-old asking who was doing car pool to school today. I recorded my emotional reactions once a week during this time (as instructed by the Bird). Each new step, each new phase took me through new reactions. Physically I felt butterflies, stomachaches and the vague symptoms of fear without specific names. I had a dull headache that lasted for two weeks, until I finished chapter One. One more block passed.

"Many memories of the past surfaced and many feelings buried came alive. I noted, about three weeks into it, that (I will quote my journal) *'when you begin writing, a certain light begins to shine in and show you things, but it is not selective. It will not just show you the things you want to see - the good stuff - it shines on everything and if you choose to turn and look at it, you will see some of what you have turned from, chose to ignore, or just was completely in shadow.'* It would have been easier to stop then look sometimes, but I was committed and I had to tell Tom every morning that I had done my 3,000 words (or more depending on his whip that day).

I had many fears that surfaced at different times. I would get weird flashes of individuals reading my writing, twisting my stomach as if they were handling me. The fear of a changed life or losing the one I had could easily stop the writing. I have a very strong faith and I knew God was showing me things with my writing and I was not going to quit. There are always reasons to stop. Writing, if it is what calls you, is part of who you are, what you are intended to be.

"I might have done this without Tom, but I know it would have taken me years and I would have not

"Style is knowing who you are, what you want and want to say, and not giving a damn."
Gore Vidal

reached the depth or understanding that I did. I have finished my first book, complete with unreadable comments by Tom in the margin; I'm ready to keep going."

He Just Couldn't Get It Together: Tom Puetz

"Success is not the result of spontaneous combustion. You must set yourself on fire."
Reggie Leach

"When writing became the main endeavor of my life, when it was clear that writing was the one thing I had to do, I went to a weekend writing seminar given by Tom Bird.

"In that first hour Tom guided me into and through a writing process that was simply amazing. It was simple and the results were amazing. Tom didn't just tell me how to write a novel. He had me doing it. Within that first hour I knew I could write my first book. The rest of the seminar was just icing on the cake. You know, the legal aspects, what literary agents do and don't do for you, how to get published, etc.

"That was four months ago. I have finished the rough draft of my first novel. I am writing the final draft and have ten thousand words written on my second novel. I could give you more details and praise Tom as a writing coach but I won't. What I will do is tell you what I feel is the truth about writing. If you believe your life is worth living, and it is, then you can believe your book is worth writing."

She Had Always Wanted To Do This But Just Didn't Know How: Kristine Larson

'There is no failure except in no longer trying."
Elbert Hubbard

"I did not always want to grow up and write a book. I have been an artist, goldsmith/designer for thirty years and am therefore very familiar with my own creative process. When the stars moved into position and called me to write some stories, I found the wise man named Tom Bird.

"Tom is a man blessed with natural grace and a gentle manner. He is not teaching me to write but is guiding me with his skilled ways into the process of writing and finding the stories within my words. Prior to meeting Tom, I had already written many pages about what I wanted to write. After meeting Tom and joining the Intensive Writer's Program, I started writing the stories. With Tom, I made the leap from ideas to stories and I have completed the first drafts of two fictional novels in two months. There are, of course, many rewrites ahead of me, but with Tom's guidance, I expect to meet the challenge of that part of the process as well, in a reasonable period of time.

"I have studied with many energy masters over the past twenty years and I can honestly say in comparison, that writing a fictional story helps one to "*peel the onion*" in a most profound way. I would recommend time with Tom to anybody interested in moving forward with their writing. He will guide you in a most creative way with his bag of tricks to keep you unstuck and writing your heart out."

Chapter Three:
Your Author Within and How Releasing It Will Change Your Life

*"Grasshopper, look beyond the game, as you look beneath the surface of the pool to see its depths."
Master Po,
Kung Fu*

You already know the connection that I am talking about. You have already experienced it thousands of times in your life. It's that invigorating, all-powerful, all seeing, all knowing connection that attaches to something way beyond yourself.

You know the one - the connection that caused you to feel as if you could have danced all night and did; when you knocked down strike after strike in rolling or nearly rolling that perfect game; when, while playing golf, the hole seemed as big as a trashcan lid; when difficult tasks at work or at home were accomplished in record times and with amazing ease, as if someone or something was working through you in guiding you to their successful completion.

You've been there. It's a common experience that we all share. You know the one, when we feel something wildly invigorating, yet strangely calming and

The Essential Connection

Have any of the following ever happened to you?

- Have you ever at any time enjoyed the act of writing?
- While taking a long drive in a car, have ideas ever flooded your mind?
- Have you ever awakened in the middle of the night with a desire to write?
- When you have gone away on a relaxing vacation have you ever gotten the strange urge to write?
- Have you ever daydreamed so deeply of writing a book or screenplay that you could actually feel yourself doing it?
- Has a story, an idea or an urge, dying to be released and calling to be written, ever stuck with you for a long time, and refused to let you go?
- Has your writing ever poured out of you so fast that you struggled to keep up with it?
- Has your writing ever had an agenda, a mind or taken on a direction its own?
- Have your spoken or written words ever carried with them a degree of intelligence or insight that you had a difficult time accepting as your own?

If you answered in the affirmative to any of the above, you are already very familiar of the connection that forms the basis of this book.

> "Everyone is in the best seat."
> John Cage

> "I can say 'I am terribly frightened and fear is terrible and awful and it makes me uncomfort-able, so I won't do that because it's uncomfort-able.' Get used to being uncomfort-able. It is uncomfort-able doing something that's risky.' But so what? Do you want to stagnate and just be comfortable?"
> Barbara Streisand

> "A musician must make music, an artist must paint, a poet must write, if he is to be ultimately at peace with himself."
> Abraham Maslow

comfortable, and widely intelligent, talented, yet beyond our human conception. This feeling can express itself through playing a game, a piano, any other instrument, or a role.

Others Who Have Experienced It

Amazing accomplishments, rates and qualities of productivity take place while in the midst of this connection.

This sensational state of connection is also not limited to any one endeavor or activity and has been experienced in every aspect of life from the arts to athletics to business to personal endeavors and interests of all sorts.

In the world of music for example, Mozart felt and welcomed it, which allowed him to brilliantly express himself through his music at an age when all other composers were still playing with blocks.

Beethoven felt it, recognized it and gave into it, which is why he was able to compose his most masterly symphony at a ripe old age, teetering on death's door, after he had gone stone deaf.

In the business arena, modern icons such as media magnate Ted Turner, the czar of the ever-expanding computer industry Bill Gates, and many others, as well, rode its calling to success and set their respective fields afire, while changing life as we know it.

In his book, *My Life and the Beautiful Game*, Pele, the great soccer player, described the state in this fashion.

"I felt a strange calmness," wrote Pele, ..."a kind of euphoria. I felt I could run all day without tiring, that I could dribble through any of their team or all of them, that I could almost pass through them physically. I felt I could not be hurt. It was a strange feeling and one I had not felt before. Perhaps it was merely confidence, but I have felt confident many times without that strange feeling of invincibility."

In the world of writing, this connection is extremely prevalent, too.

While with this connection, Jack Kerouac wrote his finest works in only a few sleepless days.

Ernest Hemmingway felt so excited and stimulated that he wrote while standing up. Thomas Wolfe did the same, and since he was so tall actually did his writing on the top of an icebox.

Samuel Beckett, the award-winning playwright, wrote his cornerstone of modern drama, *Waiting for Godot*, in a mere few months while in this state.

Singer/songwriter Harry Chapin, wrote his 1970's blockbuster hit "*Taxi*," in less than thirty minutes.

> "To love what you do and feel that it matters – how could anything be more fun?"
> Katherine Graham

You may have been there yourself, have you not, when the pen has literally jumped out of your hand, covering miles of once impassable, blank space in what felt like effortless, bliss laden seconds?

An individual student of mine, while in this state and working on the completion of her first book, wrote over 25,000 words, the equivalent of 85 double spaced pages, in one day. Another completed over 17,000 in the same period of time.

In both cases, their works, upon being edited, were found to be nearly without flaw.

I spoke to the former of the two students immediately after she had completed her day of work.

"*You must be tired,*" I probed.

> "The book should be a ball of light in one's hand."
> Ezra Pound

"*Well,*" she replied with pretty much the same spark in her voice in which she had started the day, "*I could go out dancing, I'm not too tired to go out to dinner or to attend a movie. Frankly, I am not physically, mentally or emotionally tired at all. I'm just tired of writing.*"

Common Characteristics of This Connected State While Writing

Even though this connected state is prevalent in all areas of life, nowhere is it more common and accessible by anyone, than in the world of writing.

The characteristics that one feels while connected to this state, do not vary that much from person-to-person.

"First of all, it's a daydream, a kind of rumination about a person, a situation, something that occurs only in the mind," says author Mario Vargas Llaso. "Up until now, it's been pretty much the same with all of my books. I never get the feeling that I've decided rationally, cold blooded to write a story. On the contrary, certain events or people, sometimes dreams or readings impose themselves suddenly and demand attention."

"When the language lends itself to me, when it comes and submits, when it surrenders and says – 'I am yours darling' – that's the best part," claims Maya Angelou.

"Biting my taunt pen, beating myself for spite 'Fool,' said my Muse to me, 'look in thy heart and write,'" qualified Sir Philip Sidney, 1554-1586.

"He writes as fast as they can read, and does not write himself down," spoke the author William Hazlett, 1778-1830, of the experience.

"Then rising with Aurora's light, the Muse invoked, 'sit down to write,'" adds Jonathan Swift, 1667-1745.

What Is It?

As it has been since Jackie Robinson's breaking of the color barrier, the arena of modern, big-name athletics has been the first to try and coin a title for this state of connection. Commonly referred to as the "zone," use of this title has spilled over into just about every other arena, as well.

However, no field other than writing has even attempted to consistently define what it is that we are connecting with while in this state.

"Now this creative power I think is the Holy Ghost," clarifies Brenda Ueland, author of *If You Want to Write*. "My theology may not be very accurate but that is how I think of it. I know that William Blake called this creative power the Imagination and he said that it was from God. He, if anyone, ought to know, for he was one of the greatest poets and artists that ever lived.

"There are people who have money and people who are rich."
Coco Gabrielle Chanel

"A man does not have to be an angel in order to be a saint."
Albert Schweitzer

"Tis God gives skill, but not without men's hands" He could not make Antonio Stradivari's violin without Antonio."
Stradivarius

"I'm only the Pope, what can I do?"
Pope John XXIII

Tom Bird - ~~Write~~ Right From God

"Now Blake thought that his creative power should be kept alive in all people for all of their lives and so do I. Why? Because it is life itself. It is the Spirit. In fact it is the only important thing about us. The rest of us is legs and stomach, materialistic cravings and fears."

"God has written all the books," claimed esteemed author Samuel Butler, 1835-1902.

"Language is one of those God-given gifts that we often take for granted," says Hal Zina Bennett in his book *Write From the Heart*.

Coined as an Entity

"Be bold – and mighty forces will come to your aid."
Basil King

The Greeks, Romans, and Indians had all sorts of Gods. Carl Yung created the term *archetypes*. Humans simply prefer to personify that which they feel drawn to, close to, connected with. In no other arena is that truer than writing and writers through the ages have attempted to personify that which comes through them during this most essential of all connected states.

According to Keats, the description of Apollo in the third book of his epic poem, *Hyperion*, came to him *"by chance or magic-to be, as it were, something given to me."* Keats added that he had *"not been aware of the beauty of some thought or expression until after I had composed and written it down."* It then struck him with *"astonishment"* and seemed *"rather the production of another person"* than his own.

"There exists in most men a poet who died young, when the man survived," said Saint Beuve.

"Know that there is often hidden in us a dormant poet, always young and alive," seconded de Must.

"Let us now consider the Personal Daemon....," said Rudyard Kipling. "Most men, and some most unlikely, keep him under an alias which varies with their literary or scientific attainments. Mine came to me early when I sat bewildered among other notions, and said: 'Take this and no other.' I obeyed, and was rewarded....

"Art is a collaboration between God and the artist, and the less the artist does the better."
Andre Gide

"After that I learned to lean upon him and recognize the sign of his approach. I fever I held back, Ananias fashion; anything of myself (even though I had

34

to throw it out afterwards) I paid for it by missing what I then knew the tale lacked....

"My Daemon was with me in the jungle books, Kim, and both Puck books, and good care I took to walk delicately, lest he should withdraw. I know that he did not, because when those books were finished they said so themselves with, almost, the water-hammer click of a tap turned off. Note here. When your Daemon is in charge, do not try to think consciously. Drift, wait, and obey."

In his memoirs, Robert Lewis Stevenson quite candidly personified this state as an experienced cadre of dream helpers he called his *"brownies,"* and explained how he came to use and finally to exploit them. Stevenson had a bit to say about them in a little-known essay entitled *"A Chapter on Dreams."*

"The more I think of it, the more I am moved to press upon the world my question: Who are the Little People? They are near connections of the dreamer's beyond doubt; they share in his financial worries and have an eye to the bank-book; they share plainly in his training; they have plainly learned like him to build the scheme of a considerable story and to arrange emotion in progressive order; only I think they have more talent; and one thing is beyond doubt, they can tell him a story piece by piece, like a serial, and keep him all the while in ignorance of where they aim. Who are they, then? And who is the dreamer?

"Well, as regards the dreamer, I can answer that, for he is no less a person than myself ... and for the Little People, what shall I say they are but just my Brownies, God bless them! who do one-half my work while I am fast asleep, and in all human likelihood, do the rest for me as well, when I am wide awake and fondly suppose I do it for myself. That part which is done while I am sleeping is the Brownies' part beyond contention; but that which is done when I am up and about is by no means necessarily mine, since all goes to show the Brownies have a hand in it even then. I am an excellent advisor, much like Moliere's servant. I pull back and I cut down; and I dress the whole in the best words and sentences that I can find and make; I hold the pen, too; and I do the sitting at the table, which is

---

"We need some imaginative stimulus, some not impossible ideal such as may shape vague hope, and transform it into effective desire, to carry us year after year, without disgust, through the routine work which is so large a part of life."
Walter Pater, 1885

about the worst of it; and when all is done, I make up the manuscript and pay for the registration; so that, on the whole, I have some claim to share, though not so largely as they do, in the profits of our common enterprise.

"I can but give an instance or so of what part is done sleeping and what part awake, and leave the reader to share what laurels there are, at his own nod, between myself and my collaborators; and to do this I will first take a book that a number of persons have been polite enough to read, 'The Strange Case of Dr. Jekyll and Mr. Hyde.' I had long been trying to write a story on this subject, to find a body, a vehicle, for that strong sense of man's double being which must at times come in upon and overwhelm the mind of every thinking creature. I had even written one, 'The Traveling Companion,' which was returned by an editor on the pleas that it was a work of genius and indecent, and which I burned the other day on the ground that it was not a work of genius, and that 'Jekyll' had supplanted it. Then came one of those financial fluctuations to which (with an elegant modesty) I have hitherto referred in the third person. For two days I went about racking my brains for a plot of any sort; and on the second night I dreamed the scene at the window, and a scene afterward split in two, in which Hyde, pursued for some crime, took the powder and underwent the change in the presence of his pursuers. All the rest was made awake, and consciously, although I think I can trace in much of it the manner of my Brownies."

"If we weren't all crazy, we would all go insane."
Jimmy Buffett

It is Your Essential Inspiration and Guide

"Regret for the things we did can be tempered by time; it is regret for the things we did not do that is inconsolable."
Sydney J. Harris

Depending on your chosen point of reference for understanding life, whether it be religious, psychological, scientific or romantic, that which has been described above can be coined in several ways ranging from the Heart, to the Holy Spirit, to the Muse, to the Greater Consciousness, to the Subconscious, to the Right Brain.

Even though this connection which is often times personified in the form of an entity, as mentioned previously, has far reaching capabilities and is willing to meet you wherever it is that you choose, whether that be behind a paint brush, a chisel, a keyboard, a desk, a podium or on a stage or dance floor, since we are talking solely about its essential presence in your writing, I have chosen to call it as your Author Within (AW).

You know your AW. It is the one that floods your mind with ideas when you are on a relaxing beach or mountain vacation, or when you are on a long drive by yourself in a car. It is the AW that at times awakens you in the middle of the night with an uncontrollable urge to write, who has poured out of your pen at times, causing you to appear so much more well spoken and intelligent than you see yourself.

Both of you have been awaiting this time for what seems forever. Now is the time open up, understand and appreciate your AW once and for all, and to begin to finally understand why he has come to you. Now is the time to consciously meet he or she, face-to-face, pen-to-pen, heart-to-heart.

"My dear, I don't care what they do, so long as they don't do it in the street and frighten the horses."
Mrs. Patrick Campbell

Meeting Your Author Within

Step 1. Take a moment to close your eyes and to relieve any tension that you may be feeling by taking deep breaths and blowing them out. Do this until you feel stress and worry free. This will not only relax your body, but your mind, as well, setting free any potential internal distractions.

Step 2. Once this is accomplished, it will be easy for you to go back in your mind to the time when you were your most creative. Allow that moment to come back to you in the reflection of you actually doing something creative.

How old were you at the time?

Where were you?

What was it that you were wearing?

Was anyone else there?

> *"You can have anything you want if you want it desperately enough. You must want it with an inner exuberance that erupts through the skin and joins the energy that created the world."*
> Sheila Graham

What time of year was it?

What time of day?

What was it, an incident, a person, whatever, that had caused you to want to be so creative?

What was it that you were doing?

What was it that you remember most about this incident?

Step 3. Open you eyes, pick up your pen and allow whatever it is that you feel and remember to be released on the large sheet of lineless paper before you.

Part 2:

The Problem

"Say what you will about the Ten Commandments, you must always come back to the pleasant fact that there are only ten of them."
- H.L. Mencken

"An adventure is only an inconvenience rightly considered."
- G.K. Chesterton

"One of the hardest things for any man to do is to fall down on the ice when it is wet and then get up and praise the Lord."
- Josh Billings

Chapter Four:
What Caused Your AW To Go Into Hiding All Of These Years?

"The kingdom of heaven may be compared to a man who sowed good seed in his field."
Matthew 13:24

We are all born with a seed, which I believe alludes to the link-up for the connection with our AW's, and thus the standard equipment that you need to garner the necessary understandings and direction to go on to become anything that you want to be.

"The potential for natural writing is already within all of us; it is not too late for any of us to learn," claims Gabrielle Rico in her Best Selling book *Writing the Natural Way*.

So, if you already came with the necessary communicative seed that you need to succeed, then who stops you from... becoming. The only answer that makes sense is that the only person who could stop you from doing so would be .....*You*.

Yes, the truth is that there are many outside factors that attempt to influence our free will, but we are the only ones that can keep our dreams from becoming the reality that we seek. For if outside influences were the dominate factors then persons such as Maya Angelou, who worked her way out of the ghetto and to one of the most respected writers in modern history, or Frank McCourt who rose from a severely dysfunctional upbringing to become a best selling author, and hundreds of thousands from our society who have walked the same road, as well, would have never ended up where they did.

> *"When you have to make a choice and don't make it, that in itself is a choice."*
> William James

No matter what the cost or what barriers stand between them and their dreams, some people just choose to follow that inner voice, their AW's they hear calling them forward, while others respond to another voice, that critical calling of the outside influences, that tells them to *"stand still"*, *"don't move,"* or even worse *"turn tail and run!"*

But why is it that anyone would allow this essential connection to be severed? The answer is simple. We were conditioned to do just that.

It All Begins with Society Who Tries to Sever Your Connection with Your AW

> *"The most important function of education at any level is to develop the personality of the individual and the significance of his life to himself and to others. This is the basic architecture of a life; the rest is ornamentation and decoration of the structure."*
> Grayson Kirk

It is believed that the security and strength of a society is based upon the cohesiveness of its individual members, which is, of course, based upon their abilities to fall in line, conform. Thus, even though at one time in your life, probably as a young child, you wouldn't have even considered not adhering to the expressions of your AW, eventually societal pressures, that you could not control, were brought upon you. It was then that your connection with your AW, the one which makes each one of us so unique and special, was squashed.

"The innate human need that underlies all writing, the need to give shape to your experience, is a gift we all possess from earliest childhood," says Rico.

No matter how powerful the calling of your AW and no matter how strong the connection, you were undersized, outnumbered, and out positioned, and so you had no other choice other than to give in as the first wave of severing criticism descended upon you from those who loved you and whom you depended upon the most.

> "We can secure other people's approval, if we do right and try hard; but our own is worth a hundred of it."
> Mark Twain

Parents and Others

The first attempt to get you to sever your connection with your AW came as the result of your loving parents strict adherence to and projection of society's deafening and cutting ways.

"Embarrassment, self-consciousness, remembered criticism, can stifle the average person so that less and less in his lifetime can he open himself out," says Ray Bradbury in his book The Zen of Writing.

> "Love truth, but pardon error."
> Voltaire

"That's a nice story Johnny, now go do your math homework."

"It's really cute that you like to sing Judy, but remember a nurse is what you want to be."

"Do you want to have a big house and nice car like Daddy? If you do, you better get your grades up, because artists don't make any money."

> "God sends ten thousand truths, which come about us like birds seeking inlet; but we are shut up to them, and so they bring us nothing, but sit and sing awhile upon the roof, and then fly away."
> Henry Ward Beecher

"Oh she'll grow out of it and come to her senses. She doesn't really want to be an actor. She's way to smart for that."

"I'm really worried about him Bob, he just sits there and sits there scribbling down story after story."

So few of our seeds land upon hard ground and thus are unable to survive beyond our childhoods, that they oftentimes have to wait until adulthood, when we are finally able to take off on our own.

"Only a few of us keep on expressing this need through a sustained relationship with language, our natural urge for self-expression inhibited by the weight of rules and prescriptions," concludes Rico.

> "To avoid criticism, do nothing, say nothing, be nothing."
> Elbert Hubbard

How the Educational System Further Severs Our AW Connection

The misguided influence of our society overwhelms us as we enter school, when we absorb the principles that will eventually lead us away from our AW's as the educational system, whose job it is to insure that we fit – at all costs- uses whatever influences are necessary to lower the boom.

"Every good thought you think is contributing its share to the ultimate result of your life."
Grenville Kleiser

Creating Self-Critism That Worries Over Minutia

This severing of your most intimate and necessary connection haunts us all.

"*Most of the methods of training the conscious side of the writer – the craftsman and the critic in him – are actually hostile to the good of the artist's side,*" said Dorothea Brande, in her book *Becoming a Writer*.

"*Our loss begins in school, when the process of writing is taught to us in fragments: mechanics, grammar, and vocabulary,*" says Rico. "*Writing becomes fearful and loathsome, a workbook activity. Students write as little as possible, and once out of school, they tend to avoid the entire process whenever possible. As a result, few people turn to writing as a natural source of pleasure and gratification.*

"We need some imaginative stimulus, some not impossible ideal such as may shape vague hope, and transform it into effective desire, to carry us year after year, without disgust, through the routine work which is so large a part of life."
Walter Pater, 1885

"*This is sad because children's writing naturally has an expressive power, an authenticity that inherently captures the sound of an individual on a page, an ability we seem to lose the more we learn about writing.*"

The result is a conditioned response that repulses any and all association with our AW and our expressive selves that would allow us to be whatever it was that we sought to become.

Thus the first shoe falls in the early years of our exposure to the educational system.

Misconceptions and BS

"Oh isn't life a terrible thing, thank God"
Dylan Thomas

The misinformation flows at a greater pace as we move further and farther up the educational ladder. The more formal education one acquires, the more misinformation he or she absorbs.

"A lot of people in English Departments should never be trusted to run a program," agrees Wallace Stegner. "Their training is all in the other direction, all analytical, all critical. It's all reader's training, not a writer's training, so they have no notion of how to approach the opportunity."

The higher we climb, the more inappropriate teaching and information we are expected to adhere to, all of which severs deeper, and deeper our necessary connection with our AW.

> "That old law about 'an eye for an eye' leaves everyone blind."
> Martin Luther King, Jr.

"Most books on writing are filled with bullshit," claims Best Selling Author Stephen King in his book entitled *A Memoir of the Craft On Writing*.

"Fiction writers, present company included, don't even understand very much about what they do – not why it works when it's good, not why it doesn't when it's bad," continues King.

All criticism eventually leads to unnecessary worries that initially begin to sever our relationship with our AW's, which leads to the further absorption of more misconceptions and as King would coin it, "*bullshit*", which eventually creates unnecessary fears, including even of what we want most in life.

Chapter Five: Fears

Fear of Success

"Beloved, I wish above all things that thou mayest prosper and be in health, even as thy soul prospereth." 3 John 1:2

When I began teaching, I decided to put my background in psychology to work by surveying my students in regard to that which they feared most about being expressive via their writing. Much to my surprise, the majority of persons who I surveyed feared what they wanted most: the ultimate form of expression, as they knew it – the successful completion and sale of their books. Of course, in a perfect or a functional world, such events would be greeted with open arms, not distain, disbelief, and concern. However, this is not the case in our world where failure is the accepted mode of experience.

Thus, if you are anything at all like the population represented in that survey, even though the alteration in your expressive life style may bring you everything that you personally sought, you may fear a loss of your privacy and anonymity that may come with it, as well.

You may worry that if you become a writer, or what-

> "I believe that anyone can conquer fear by doing the things he fears to do, provided he keeps doing them until he gets a record of successful experiences behind him."
> Eleanor Roosevelt

> "Pain is inevitable. Suffering is optional."
> M. Kathleen Casey

ever it is that you truly want to be in your life, that your friends, spouses, and family, with whom your relationships are conditional, would no longer like or love you, or vice versa. All of this would come as the result of your connection with your AW, which once again frees you to express, who you really are. You could also fear the reprisals that would come as a result.

Where would dysfunctional reactions such as these come from? They come from the constant connection with a controlling and condescending society, and all those who have been exposed to it, including our family and friends, our business associates and those we have come in contact with through the educational system. Thus, it is no wonder that the possibility of having what it is that we want most has actually at times repulsed us from attempting to acquire it.

Below are some of the typical responses I received to my survey.

> **All of this manifests in two forms, as:**
> - *Fear of change.*
> - *Fear of losing friends.*

> "A good memory is one trained to forget the trivial."
> Clifton Fadiman

Examples of Fears of Success

Fears of Change

> "Hope is the feeling you have that the feeling you have isn't permanent."
> Jean Kerr

"If I succeed at writing, I will be expected to continue to do so, and I'm not sure that I will be able to follow through. In fact, I'm not even sure that I have a book in me, let alone others. So wouldn't it be just a whole heck of a lot easier to avoid all of the embarrassment and hassle by not even attempting to write in the first place?"

"Hey, I've been living the same style of life for as

long as I can remember. I've had the same job for years. I've lived in the same house and the same town for what seems like forever. My life may not be everything I want it to be, but no one can guarantee me that it wouldn't be a heck of a lot worse were I to risk it in going after what it is that I think I really want."

"Successful authors are always on the go. They're always writing something, touring here or there. They have wealth and esteem. Everybody knows them, and I'm just not cut out for all that stuff."

"People will know more about me than I am comfortable with them knowing."

> "One should sympathize with the joy, the beauty, the color of life – the less said about life's sores the better."
> Oscar Wilde

"I'll be seen as being crazy."

"I will look like a fool."

"The world likes the little guy. It's the guy with all the money and fame that it dislikes. Assassinations are reserved for those with power and fame. No one has ever heard of a nobody being attacked for who they were."

Fears of Loss

"Those closest to me just won't understand me any more, and there's nothing that I value more than their company, attention and affection."

> "Statistically, the probability of any one of us being here is so small that you'd think the mere fact of existing would keep us all in a contented dazzlement of surprise."
> Lewis Thomas

"If I end up where it is that I want to go, for the first time in my life I will have something in my life that I will love and thus I will fear losing it."

"My life may be far from perfect, but at least I am in control of it. If I were to succeed at my writing, there is no doubt that I would lose the structure I need to live, exist, and that is just not acceptable."

"I will be hounded by all sorts of responsibilities. I will no longer have my own time, my own life."

"I will be overtaken by my love for my writing and I won't be able to continue to fulfill my obligations to those around me. As a result, they will eventually end up disliking me or possibly even leaving me."

"I would have to leave those I love, to do what I want to do."

Examples of Fears of Failure

Since these fears are typically beat into our heads at a young age, you may relate to many of the following, which form the initial line of repulsion to our AW. It is, of course, only after you break through these barriers that you are awarded with the opportunity to experience the former.

Fears of Failure fall into primarily one category.

Fears of Lack

"No one would be interested in what I'd have to say or do anyway."

"Anything that I would try on my own wouldn't work."

"No matter what I do I always wind up screwing up."

"I have a difficult time believing that I deserve anything good in my life."

"I'm not smart enough."

"I don't have enough money."

"I'm not attractive enough."

"I'm not brave enough."

"I'm not dedicated enough."

"I'm not serious enough."

"I don't have good luck."

"I haven't paid my dues."

"I'm not talented enough."

"How often – even before we began – have we declared a task 'impossible'? And how often have we construed a picture of ourselves as being inadequate?—a great deal depends upon the thought patterns we choose and on the persistence with which we affirm them."
Piero Ferrucci

"If we had no winter; the spring would not be so pleasant; if we did not sometimes taste of adversity, prosperity would not be so welcome."
Anne Bradstreet, 1664

Tom Bird - ~~Write~~ *Right From God*

"I'm too old."

"I'm too young."

"I don't have anything to say."

"Who would want to hear what I have to say anyway?"

The Man or Woman in the Mirror: The Good News is that You Can Reverse It

"Adam was human; he didn't want the apple for the apple's sake; he wanted it because it was forbidden."
Mark Twain

It is up to you to decide what it is that you will do with your life. Now is the time to take back that control and move swiftly and joyfully forward in the direction of your dreams and aspirations. Just like a light socket responds only to a certain type of bulb, you won't be able to make the necessary connection with your AW unless you begin seeing yourself as it sees you.

The following exercise is designed to enable you to do just that. For it, you will need a mirror. You are to stay with this exercise until you can look yourself in the eye and feel nothing at all in response to the following statements. Then, and only then will the effects of the previous conditionings be cleansed from your psyche. Then, and only then will you be prepared to move forward. For some of you, this may mean a pass or two through the exercise. For others, it may mean dozens of runs through. There is no right or wrong in regards to the numbers of times you move through the following. All that matters is that the damage of the past is cleared out and your wounds are healed for good. Let's begin.

"No time like the present."
Mary De La Riviere Manley, 1696

Step 1. Find yourself in front of a mirror.

Step 2. Take time to close your eyes, clear your mind and relax.

Step 3. Then, using the mirror, look yourself directly in the eye and repeat the first statement, allowing any and all thoughts or feelings, whether

"In the depth of winter, I finally learned that within me there lay an invincible summer."
Albert Camus

they are tied directly to your writing or not, that arise to spill out onto your paper. After you have done that, repeat the statement again and allow whatever it is that arises to spill out on the paper again. Do this over and over and over again, even if it takes several sessions or many days, until you can look yourself in the eye, repeat the statement and feel nothing. Then move onto the next statement and do the same thing. Once you have completed your work with statement number two, then follow the same exact steps with the third statement, and the fourth and then the fifth and final one. Do not move on to the next section until you have verified that you can look at yourself in the eye and repeat any of the five statements and feel nothing.

Five Statements

1) *"Life is my best teacher; it provides me with all that I need to know."*

2) *"My mind is an endless storehouse of ideas and inspirations."*

"A short saying oft contains much wisdom."
Sophocles

3) *"I do best what I like to do most."*

4) *"What I like to do most brings me the personal success that I desire."*

5) *"What I like to do most affords me all the opportunities I desire to live my life as I choose."*

Chapter Six:
The Eighteen CBs

"Let is be thankful for the fools but for them the rest of us could not succeed."
Mark Twain

"Fear is that little darkroom where negatives are developed."
Michael Pritchard

The inappropriate schoolings we received from our friends, families, the educational system, and society has caused us to generate our own writing related fears. I have broken these into eighteen separate areas, I refer to as Connection Breakers (CBs), because they sever the connection between the natural abilities of our AW's and us.

A listing of these 18 CBs are as follows:

Connection Breaker Number One:
Only special or chosen persons are born with the ability to make this most special of all connections.

Connection Breaker Number Two:
It is up to this connection to choose if and when it ever visits, and more importantly – who it visits.

> "To conquer fear is the beginning of wisdom."
> Bernard Russell

> "To see a world in a grain of sand and heaven in a wild flower, to hold infinity in the palm of your hand and eternity in an hour."
> William Blake

> "Mistakes are the portals of discovery."
> James Joyce

> "You have to leave the city of your comfort and go into the wilderness if your intuition. What you'll discover will be wonderful. What you'll discover will be yourself."
> Alan Alda

Connection Breaker Number Three:
Not everyone has something to say.

Connection Breaker Number Four:
Writing is difficult, demanding.

Connection Breaker Number Five:
You should always know what you are writing.

Connection Breaker Number Six:
Not everyone has a major project in them.

Connection Breaker Number Seven:
The past determines the future.

Connection Breaker Number Eight:
To be a writer you need to be a reader.

Connection Breaker Number Nine:
You need to be committed to do any good with your writing.

Connection Breaker Number Ten:
One should write on lined pads of paper or on a typewriter or via a computer word processing program.

Connection Breaker Number Eleven:
Always stay within the lines of what it is that you are writing about.

Connection Breaker Number Twelve:
To produce good writing one has to carefully search for mistakes as he or she goes.

Connection Breaker Number Thirteen:
You shouldn't leave gaps and guesses in your writing.

Connection Breaker Number Fourteen:
It is a bad idea to stop writing before you have completed a scene or section.

Connection Breaker Number Fifteen:
You have to be highly educated in spelling, grammar and syntax to be a good writer.

Connection Breaker Number Sixteen:
It takes forever to write a book or screenplay.

Connection Breaker Number Seventeen:
Writers are responsible for "creating" books.

Connection Breaker Number Eighteen:
That to be a successful writer, you need to edit and edit and edit your work over and over and over again.

"It is hard to fight an enemy who has outposts on your head."
Sally Kempton

The Logical / Critical Mind

Our immense exposure to the effects of these CBs has transformed an ally into an adversary. For in response to the fears associated with the above CBs, the critical side of our logical minds was created. It is this side of our brains that has become hyper vigilant in keeping us away from any potential pain or danger, both of which it associates with the AW, and any form of expression, including writing, that we may attempt to release from the AW.

Part 3:

Solutions

"Mr. Spock: May I point out that I had an opportunity to observe your counterparts quite closely. They were brutal, savage, unprincipled, uncivilized, treacherous – in every way, splendid examples of Homo Sapiens. The very flower of humanity. I found them quite refreshing. Captain Kirk (to Dr. McCoy): I'm not sure, but I think we've been insulted.
- Star Trek

"O ye Gods grant us what is good whether we pray for it or not, but keep evil from us even though we pray for it."
- Plato

"Nothing can be attained without suffering but at the same time one must begin by sacrificing suffering."
- Gurudjieff

Chapter Seven:
The Three R's of Writing

"Do or do not. There is no try." Yoda

One hundred percent of your success as both a human being and as an author, is directly tied to your ability to consistently connect with your AW. What has kept us from being able to do this as freely and easily, as we did as children, are the learned associations and habits, that we have picked up along the way from our families, friends, our education and society as a whole. So routinized have these become over the course of our lives that we no longer think when it comes to the topic of writing, feeling or expressing, we just react.

"We are not interested in the possibilities of defeat." Queen Victoria

You know exactly what I am talking about. Have you ever set a specific date and time to do an expressive activity such as writing or to have that big intimate talk with a spouse, lover or family member, or that major discussion with your boss or business partner about a raise or something that is bothering you? If so, you may have experienced one of the most common knee-jerk reactions. Did you notice that the closer you came to one of these specific dates or times the more important routine chores and responsibilities became? Why do you think this happened?

Or in the first writing exercise that we did together, when you visualized the time when you were creative, looking back, what were the reasons that you either moved back from or didn't follow through on the creative activities that you wanted to do at that time? Can you recall? Take a few moments to do so before moving on.

Do you recall one of these times when you actually did sit down to express at an appointed time and place, and found yourself under a barrage of phone calls and worries and distractions?

Can you recall times when you were creating but when you seemed to be interrupted over an over again, by your own concerns?

If so, during either of these times, did you notice that the more you fretted over your work the slower and slower the material continued to flow, until it may have either slowed to a crawl or stopped for good?

How about when you did have one of those expressive sessions when the feeling just seemed to flow out of you? Do you remember coming back to whatever it was that you did or said somewhere in the near to distant future and having either an adverse or less than appreciative reaction to what happened during that time which was so pleasing to you when it was initially released?

Each of the above circumstances are typical examples of disconnectiveness with your AW and came as the result of one of the eighteen *Connection Breakers* (CBs).

"There's nothing to winning really. That is, if you happen to be blessed with a keen eye, an agile mind, and scruples whatsoever." Alfred Hitchcock

> **These CBs sever your necessary connection with your AW by either:**
>
> - Attempting to keep you from expressing, via a wide variety of interruptions and excuses.
> - Disconnecting you from your AW after you've already begun to express by convincing you to doubt the validity of whatever it is that you are doing
> - Destroying any and all of the substance of what it was that you did or said by editing your experience or output into oblivion.

"Laziness is nothing more than the habit of resting before you get tired."
Jules Penard

However, anyone can connect with the part of the brain that allows you to commune with your AW. All you need to do to dislodge the societal effects that you have grown used to, but dissatisfied with, is to consistently put into play the *Three R's of Writing*.

In school you were taught the three Rs of reading, 'riting, 'rithmatic. Now you are going to learn a new three Rs that will undo the damage caused by the way you were taught to approach writing.

The *Three Rs* allow you to naturally get in touch with your AW by undoing the blocking effects brought on by the first three *Connection Breakers*.

"People hate me because I am a multifaceted, talented, wealthy, intentionally famous genius."
Jerry Lewis

Connection Breakers #1-3

Connection Breaker Number One:
Only special or chosen persons are born with the ability to make this most special of all connections.

Most people who have something to say and feel the urgings of their AW, never try to express them because they believe they aren't special enough to be heard or weren't tapped by birth or fate with the special qualities that it supposedly takes to be a worthy of being heard. How many times have you told yourself that you're just not one of the blessed ones, that you shouldn't waste your time attempting to express your deepest inspirations. Yet, the urge to express refuses to leave you alone.

Every one of the over 50,000 students who have walked into my class the last eighteen years have felt the exact same way. They showed up not because they knew they could write, but because they wanted to write.

Thus I always begin by attacking their doubting, sometimes paralyzing effects, of CB #1. I do so by immediately taking them through the *Three R's* and instantly, once connected with their AW's, they begin writing like the authors that they truly *already* are.

Thousands of these students went onto get published, a huge percentage of them completed manuscripts.

If *"only special persons are born with the ability to express,"* this would not have been the case for such a wide variety of persons of all ages, educational levels, races and backgrounds.

The same success will happen for you as you move steadily through this book. In fact, you have already touched a bit of this success via the writing exercises you have done up to this point.

Not only were you able to self induce a connection with your AW, but the expressive individual that you already are will flow out of you immediately afterward. If CB #1 would have had even the least amount of validity, this would not have been possible, not only for you but so many others, as well.

"Universities should be safe havens where ruthless examination of realities will not be distorted by the aim to please or inhibited by the risk of displeasure."
Kingman Brewster

Connection Breaker Number Two:
It is up to this connection to choose if and when it ever visits, and more importantly - who it visits.

You've heard the old canard embodied in the above. You can't just sit down and write when you want. You have to wait for inspiration, that magical connection with your AW, to strike. So you wait, and you wait and you wait. And finally, you got tired of waiting and you picked up this book.

One thing is clear: there is something inside you that won't leave you alone, which comes to you in the oddest of times, like when you are driving alone in a car and the ideas literally pour out of you, or when they wake you up in the middle of the night crying to be shared.

Instances such as these and many others prove that there is indeed a Muse, which I refer to as your AW, that is trying to contact you. It just comes at the most inconvenient times.

The times when it does appear, actually correlates with your unknown and innocent, yet direct, application of the *Three R's* which follow.

If connecting with one's AW were so involuntary and damned impossible, then none of the tens of thousands of my students would have been able to do what they did within fifteen minutes of entering my classroom.

> *"Creative minds always have been known to survive any kind of bad training."*
> Anna Freud

To the contrary of CB #2, as has been proven hundreds of times in your life when the inspiration has struck, your AW is just waiting for you to make the necessary connection. You have accidentally done so on hundreds, if not thousands of occasions, when in depth inspirations just came pouring through. Now, all you need to know, is how to go about actualizing those steps on your own, which is exactly what this chapter is all about.

Connection Breaker Number Three:
Not everyone has something to say.

> *"Only the hand that erases can write the true thing."*
> Meister Echart

Can you recall when you were in one of those expressive modes somewhere in the past when the feelings seemed to just flow out of you? While there, you probably felt a sense of exhilaration yet calmness. You may have even been surprised by the intelligence and worldliness of your prose and what it had to say as it flowed out of you. Remember?

The awe-inspiring uniqueness that you may have felt is a typical characteristic of the AW. It is what makes you special and what you say and do special, as well.

It is what also gives whatever it is that you write while connected to the AW newness and importance, completely disproving the validity of CB #3.

All you have to do is connect, sit down, and write. Your AW, and the newness and importance of the message that it brings with it, will do the rest.

The Three R's of Writing

The remedy for the damage done to our connection with our AW by these three Connection Busters is what I call the *Three R's of Writing*.

"I have seen you in the sanctuary and beheld your power and your glory."
Psalm 63:2

The catalyst for the composition of my *Three R's* of Writing was the work done by Nobel Prize winning physician Roger W. Sperry and his colleagues at the California Institute of Technology.

As Sperry was able to illustrate through his Split Brain Theory, each one of us has a creative center in our brains, which I refer to as our AW. Sperry also illustrated that connecting with this creative side of your brain can be accomplished through entering into a specific state.

That's where the *Three R's of Writing* come into play, restoring that connection by removing the limiting effects of CBs #1-3.

In short, the *Three R's* desensitize the parts of our brain that house the reactive tendencies of the first three CBs, allowing direct and immediate access through the film of misconception and to an instant connection with your AW. If applied on a consistent basis, I promise that you will never again suffer from any of the debilitating effects tied to the first three CBs.

"The man who fears suffering is already suffering from what he fears."
Michel de Montaigne

Once The Three R's of Writing are employed:

- *The expressive writing state that may have drawn you to the art of writing in the first place will return and be available to you at your beck and call.*

- *The feelings, thoughts, and inspirations that have made your writing so captivating in the past will be yours at will.*

- *Your unique voice, insights, and message will come bursting through.*

- *Any strain of writer's block that you may be suffering from, or that you had ever been plagued with, will be cured immediately.*

- *You'll be able to sit down and write at your effective best any time and anywhere that you choose.*

- *As a result, you will no longer waste hours, weeks, months, and years waiting for the Muse to arrive; you'll be able to begin now and the time that you do reserve for writing you will spend writing and not waiting.*

- *The words of whatever has been bugging you to express, will begin effortlessly spilling out of you.*

- *As a result of all of the above, you will become aware that there is a unique, interesting, thought provoking, potentially awe-inspiring message coming through you, that you can access, enjoy, release and share at will.*

- *Because of the effectiveness of The Three R's, expressing, and especially writing, will become fun, stimulating and exciting.*

> **The Three R's of Writing stand for:**
>
> - *Reserving time.*
> - *Removing all outside distractions.*
> - *Relaxing.*

"Charity begins at home."
Terence, 190-159 B.C.

'R' Number One:
Reserve time to write.

"I'm just too busy." "I barely get done what I need to do in a day." "There's just no time!"

Have you ever tried to listen to two persons attempting to talk to you at the same time about two totally different subjects? How successful were you in doing so? Not very, I'm sure.

You have one set of ears that can only focus on one voice or audio task at a time. If you attempt to focus on something else while your AW's voice is attempting to come through, you not only won't be able to hear what your Author Within is attempting to share but you won't be able to do a very good job of concentrating on the other voice or task, as well.

Thus, to be able to comfortably and effectively hear what your AW has to share, make sure to reserve a time when your sole intent will be to listen to he or she.

"He is his own best friend, and takes delight in privacy; whereas the man of no virtue or ability is his own worst enemy and is afraid of solitude."
Aristotle

How much time is necessary? Start with an hour a day, six days a week at the beginning. Then, gradually increase the amount of time after a week to an extra five minutes a day until you wind up writing a minimum of two hours a day, six days a week.

My own experiences, as well as interviews with hundreds of writers, suggest the most productive time to write is in the middle of the night. The connection to our AW's appears to be a lot less busy during that time. That's when the critical side of your mind, the side that retains all of the CBs, is asleep which makes it much easier to communicate with your AW without interference. In fact, many writers, and as mentioned, you may have experienced this yourself, are often awakened by flashes of inspiration at night.

Writing in the middle of the night is not always the most convenient time, though. The most convenient time to schedule your daily writing sessions for communing with your AW is as soon after you arise from your day or night's sleep as possible. The critical side of your mind is still half-asleep. There are other benefits, as well. Your energy level will be high, which is a plus because you will best be able to resist the concerns of your critical side. And, by making writing your first activity of the day, connecting with your AW, you will have a lot less stress because you will be removing the anxiety that enters your life as the result of not releasing your Author Within. Less stress means starting out your morning in the proper frame of mind, and thus having a much, much, much better chance of having a great day.

Consistency is paramount to your success. Schedule writing sessions, of no less than an hour in length, in advance six days a week, and stick to them.

> *"How beautiful it is to do nothing and then to rest afterward.*
> Spanish Proverb

'R' Number Two:
Removing all outside distractions.

Been there, done that? Just about every one has at one time or another, whether they were dealing with writing or some other nearly equally important real-to-life activity.

The reason for the necessity to remove all chances of outside distractions that could interrupt your writing and thus your connecting with your AW is obvious. If you allow the outside world to enter your sacred writing space at will, you will never get to write. Bar the door, disconnect the phone and warn those you live with, and mean it, or else the consistency you need and the expression you seek will never become a reality. Period.

Any place you choose to write will actually do -- a hotel room, den, dining room, bedroom, even the backseat of a car will suffice as long as the above distraction free requirements are met.

> *"To feel themselves in the presence of true greatness many men find it necessary only to be alone."*
> Tom Masson

Tom Bird - ~~Write~~ Right From God

> **Scheduling your writing later in the day reduces your degree of effectiveness drastically. The reasons for that are:**
>
> - *That the part of your mind that houses the CBs will have become fully awake and active by then;*
> - *With social obligations, business and family responsibilities, those times are much more difficult to corner for your writing.*
> - *You will have expended your best energy by later in the day.*

"We may affirm absolutely that nothing great in the world has been accomplished without passion." Hegel, 1832

'R' Number Three:
Relax.

The key to being able to connect with your AW comes through relaxing, which is why it has been so difficult for us to make the necessary connection with our Authors Within during times of Writer's Block. The more and more frustrated or angry or scared we became, the farther and farther it moved us away from the relaxation we actually need to dull our critical sides and gain the sought after connection with our AW's.

"We must reserve a back shop all our own, entirely free, in which to establish our real liberty and our principal retreat and solitude." Michel Eyquem de Montaigne

This necessary state of relaxation has been there every time you have accidentally or innocently connected with your AW in the past. When you were taking that long drive in the car and all of a sudden your mind was flooded with ideas, what happened to cause it? With nothing else to do and no one else to worry about, you slipped into your long-distance driving mode and you ... relaxed! When you relaxed, the critical side of your mind which is very human and thus known to nod off at times, did what? Went to sleep, allowing your squashed AW to finally come bursting into your consciousness.

The same situation was emulated if you have been awakened in the middle of the night with a desperate need to write. Sleep is an extreme form of relaxation, which lulled your critical side off to sleep, allowing your AW to finally break through with a very important insight for you.

The vacation at the beach, in the mountains, or that long plane flight home when all kinds of ideas flooded your consciousness? The same exact thing was happening.

So how do you relax? That is completely and totally up to you. You can meditate, take a catnap, do some yoga, take a walk. The best technique that I know of for achieving the necessary state of relaxation is through the use of the step-by-step routine you have already been introduced to through the exercises in this book. If you consistently utilize that routine you will always be able to fully and totally connect with your AW.

Whatever method you choose though, make sure to set aside time to relax before beginning to write. Otherwise, your critical side will always be in the way of you gaining the necessary connection with your AW.

These three steps, when followed consistently, will undo the harm caused by the influence of CBs #1-3. You will find yourself in touch with your AW more easily. This will enable you to write freer, more expressively than you ever thought possible, faster and more competently as you and your AW are once again reunited for the living of your life purpose.

Ben Cartwright: I'm not in the habit of giving lectures, and if I do, it's because they're needed. Might have been a good idea if your father had given you a few.
Candy Canaday: Oh, he did.
Ben: Obviously they didn't have much effect.
Candy: Oh, yes they did; I left home.
Bonanza

The Semi-Round Room and the Elevator Ride to the Top

Step 1. After following essential steps to prepare for the necessary relaxation that this exercise calls for, allow the image to appear in your mind of yourself during the time, which you related to previously as your most expressive.

Step 2. This time see that image of yourself standing in front of an elevator door waiting for it to open. You're alone. The area in which you stand is empty except for you; your favorite music is playing in the background.

Step 3. Visualize the door opening to an empty elevator, with the exception of a tall director's chair with your name stenciled on the back of it. You step inside and ease into the chair. As you do, the door closes behind you and the elevator rises slowly and comfortably to the very top of its shaft, where the door opens once again, this time to reveal someone that you feel very close to who is waiting for you.

Visualize this person stepping inside the elevator, giving you a big, loving bear hug, lifting you out of the chair, gently taking you by the arm and escorting you out of the elevator and down a long hallway toward a set a double doors.

Once through the doors, you step into a large amphitheater type room, with every seat filled. Once those in the seats see you entering into the room, they all rise to their feet and begin to clap and cheer.

You stop for a moment, as all of this jubilation is taking place, to look around the room. Some of the persons you recognize as those who believed in you and helped you along the way. They are the minority though. For the rest are made up of all kinds of people who you do not recognize: young, old, wealthy, poor, attractive and not so. Some are Americans, some are not. Some are Anglo, some African-American, some Native Americans. All different types of persons are present.

The person who met you at the elevator then

> "Forget goals. Value the process."
> Jim Bouton

> "The latter part of a wise man's life is taken up in curing the follies, prejudices, and false opinions he had contacted in the former."
> Jonathan Swift

leads you onto a rise in the center of the room before your applauding audience. Once there, the cheering of the crowd rises as he or she bends down to pick up something for you which most represents whatever it is that you are called to write, and hands it to you.

You take a moment to enjoy the weight of it in your hands. Gaze at it.

If you want a place in the sun you must leave the family tree.
Osage Saying

Step 4. Open your eyes, pick up your pen and allow however it is that you feel to pour out of you. Remember to blow out any and all tension you may feel and to re-relax if necessary as many times as necessary until the message has thoroughly and completely expressed all that you feel.

"I am in the present. I cannot know what tomorrow will bring forth. I can know only what the truth is for me today. That is what I am called upon to serve, and I serve it in all lucidity."
Igor Stravinsky, 1936

Chapter Eight:
How Your AW Speaks to You or Through You and, if You're a Writer, to Your Readers

I am sure that you have remembered your dreams at one time or another. At times, your dreams may have even been so alive that they awoke you from a very deep and sound sleep, leaving you with an overwhelming conscious impression or feeling. That is a very accurate example of your AW trying to get through to you.

With these images, some sort of feeling(s) associated with it caused you to react in one manner or another. These images, which allow you to feel something, are how your AW communicates with you.

Understanding Your Archetypes

"I came to the conclusion that one of the reasons why I'm so blessed, I think, is because I reach so many people, and you never know whose life you are touching or affecting. And so, because your blessings come back to you based upon how you give them out...that's why I'm so...You know what I'm saying? You get it? Okay, good."
Oprah Winfrey

Famous psychotherapist Carl Jung first coined the images of our subconscious, or in this case our AW, as archetypes.

For our intents and purposes, archetypes are best defined as *"symbolic representations of deeper universal meaning and/or communications."* Read this definition over a few times again to enable it to sink in.

You have been influenced by archetypes pouring through other persons, especially authors and others in the arts, your entire life.

Remember the famous screen character of Rocky? Whom did he represent on a deeper level? The *"have nots."*

How about *West Side Story*? The Jets and the Sharks were universal symbolic representations of what? The *"haves and have nots."* In both cases these archetypes were created by and projected through whom? The author's AW.

On the non-fiction end, archetypes are just as prevalent but not nearly as obvious to us as their fictional counterparts. However, they are there and they are just as essential to forming the necessary heart bond between AW – author and reader.

Take for example the best selling series of books by John Gray, *Men are from Mars and Women are from Venus*. Gray's archetypical reflections are mirror images of whom? Our ever-growing singles culture and their wants, needs, desires and inefficiencies.

All archetypes, no matter whether they appear in the form of a theme, design or character, represent deeper, universal meanings. Even math as an archetype when passed through someone as AW connected as Albert Einstein can reflect a way of looking at life, the Earth and everything that goes along with it.

Beyond the very obvious, why then is this important to you? Because the writing exercise that you previously completed was stocked full of all types of archetypes that can share with you mountains of information about yourself, and everything else your AW is trying to move through you, as well.

The Two Types of Archetypes

My extensive experience has caused me to break the archetypes that could and do appear as the result of your AW association into two distinctly different categories which will enable you to much better understand what is being shared with you and why by your AW.

Transformational Archetypes

Even though all writing and expression is always transformational in one way or another, this form of archetype exists for the sold purpose of *transforming you* and nothing else.

Common Characteristics of the Transformational Archetype

Number One, Transformational Archetypes all surface in the form of a thing, a person, or an animal, fish or bird that we trust. In most cases, we love this person, entity or thing. If it is capable, it loves us too and does not threaten us in any manner, way or form.

Trust the main component in this type of association. Remember that an archetype's sole purpose is communication, and this form of communicator will be coming to you on a very close and dear, personal level. So it is essential that you trust this image before you will be willing to listen to what he, she, or it has to say.

Number Two, *Transformational Archetypes appear, for one reason or another, to educate you through the removal of bias.* You may want to read that statement again, to insure that it sinks in fully.

Oftentimes and actually in most cases, the bias that I refer to is against ourselves. The removal of this bias-based barrier is essential in order to permit the release of any books or screenplays that have been dying to be expressed through you.

For example, the family member, close friend or

"America's best buy is a telephone call to the right man."
Ilka Chase

"Wealth is not in making money, but in making the man while he is making the money."
John Wicker

> "If a man is in health, he doesn't need to take anybody else's temperature to know where he is going."
> Elwyn Brooks White

associate who met you on the outside of the elevator was probably someone you loved or cared for, or even more importantly, who unconditionally loved and/or cared for you. Why then would this specific individual appear? The answer to that question lies in the fact that he, she, or it appeared to reflect back to you that which you have either forgotten or don't see in or about yourself. Why is this so important? It is so important because it allows you to finally begin removing your own personal barriers that could hold you back from accepting all the beauty, depth, and expression that has been and will soon be coming through you.

Why is it necessary for the love and/or affection projected toward you by this archetype be unconditional? First, it is necessary that it be unconditional because all love and affection is either unconditional or it is not sincere love and affection. Second, because the unconditionality of the affection, once accepted by us, allows us to accept it for ourselves and thus enables us to accept the essential connection with our AWs. Third, the acceptance of ourselves needs to be unconditional because it then allows us to accept whatever it is that comes to us from our AW. And since that sort of experience more often than not removes the dark blinders by which we try to gaze through onto life and ourselves, it is essential for our own sanities and levels of joy.

Number Three, *Transformational Archetypes rarely ever wind up as characters or representations of themes in whatever it is that you may choose to write.* Of course, there are the occasional exceptions to this rule when the author chooses to release a necessary cathartic expression in the form of a book. Wondrous examples of this rarity abound throughout literary history, including the work of Frank McCourt and his best seller *Angela's Ashes*.

However, this is not necessary and not necessarily functional to do so, for there is a risk involved with this form of expression, especially if it is the author's initial work. If an author on his or her first book releases a cathartic work such as *Angela's Ashes*, he or she automatically, no matter how successful or unsuccessful the work, accepts this form of writing as reflective of his or her style. Acceptance of this form of one time writing as one's true style also makes it nearly impossible for this sort of author to move into other projects that await he or she, which will most certainly fall outside of the structure and expression of their initial work.

This sort of dilemma has transpired into the concept of the "one book author." We all have a story to tell in this regard, when we fell madly in love with an author's first work and couldn't wait for his or her next work to come flying down the literary pipeline. However, where the disappointment comes in is when this author's next works fall dramatically short of the impact, style and voice of his or her first and only masterpiece.

So to avoid this dilemma on your own end, it is important to keep in mind that Transformational Archetypes (TA) exist solely to educate us about ourselves, or whatever else it is that we need to know, so that any barriers or bias that may stand in-between us and our AWs can be removed for good.

Lastly, it is important to keep in mind that if more than one transformational archetype is needed to complete the job of removing all that stands between you and your AW, that you will be moved from listening to one character to being addressed by another familiar reflection from your life.

Typically, if more than one Transformational Archetype is needed, the first will appear all by his or herself. After he or she has made the point that was necessary, then the first appearing transformational character will disappear as quickly as he, she, or it initially popped into your life and either another TA or a Primary Archetype (PA) will storm in to take its place. If the later takes place, that denotes for you the conclusion of the TA experience and the transferring of your writing into the realm of the PA based experience.

Primary Archetypes

Primary Archetypes (PA) are vastly different from their TA counterparts.

For one, whether you are a writer or writing to

"The best way out is always through."
Robert Frost

"He is not busy being born he is busy dying."
Bob Dylan

"It's all right to have butterflies in your stomach. Just get them to fly in formation."
Dr. Rob Gilbert

> "What seems nasty, painful, evil, can become a source of beauty, joy and strength. If faced with an open mind. Every moment is a golden one for him who has the vision to recognize it as such."
> Henry Miller

> "The writer's only responsibility is to his art. He will be completely ruthless if he is a good one. He has a dream. Everything goes by the board; honor, pride, decency, security, happiness, all to get the book written. If a writer has to rob his mother, he will not hesitate; the 'Ode on a Grecian Urn' is worth any number of old ladies."
> William Faulkner

release the true you, PAs appear in your writing in the form of someone or something you either don't know or do not recognize. That, of course, is one of the most shocking yet exhilarating attributes of PAs. Shocked but wildly excited is how I would best categorize my students' typical reaction to the initial appearance of a PA in their writing.

When I work with a student through my *Intensive Writing Program*, he or she is responsible for checking in with me at an allotted time six days a week. A student who I am currently retained by, called me one day during her appointed time and told me that she began hearing a woman's voice in her head during her writing time, and that the lady was speaking to her in an English accent. Concerned, but curious, my student wasn't quite sure what to do.

Having been through the experience myself and with my students thousands of times, I knew exactly what was happening. My student had turned the corner on the cathartic end of her writing and she was now ready to go head long into the writing of her tale. How did I surmise this? Because as you will see from the further definitions that follow, that person calling out to her was a PA, probably her protagonist, who is usually the first to appear.

The student to which I am referring to was highly educated, a Ph.D. psychotherapist. Those with advanced degrees oftentimes, because of their training, can be overly critical of the AW. So they often need a little nudge to insure they move in the correct direction. She was no different. In fact, she was the first of three students that week, Another was a psychiatrist and the other was a holder of a master's degree, with whom I needed to apply the same actions I eventually took with the former.

So I gave this student of mine a name by which she could refer to her voice, as well as another name and a slight physical description for a male counterpart. I also offered her a few areas in which I suggested she explore the identity of these two individuals, why they had come together, and what it was that they were meant to do as a tandem.

Responding to what I assumed was a natural calling of her AW, the student leapt right into the exercise the next day, and the female voice, having gained the acceptance and opening she craved, came pouring through. Immediately, my student found herself completely immersed in the background and voice of the character. Within no time at all, she knew more about this woman, who was more than happy to answer whatever questions were posed to her, than she did about most of her clients. This woman, who was obviously my student's protagonist, was now where she needed to be, in full control. After having seized control of the situation, the female PA renamed her male counterpart and told my student all that she could possibly want to know about herself, him and the story that they were going to write together.

    This is not an uncommon occurrence. In fact, most of you have probably already experienced this in one way or another with your dreams already. The simple reason that this form of communication may not have worked for you as well as you have wanted it to up to this point, comes directly as the result of not understanding, and thus being able to give into, that which came pouring through you so naturally. This lack of understanding about what was actually taking place, caused you, in one way or another, to panic, which in turn called forth your critical logical mind, which shut down your entire connection with your AW.

    Somewhere along the way, as well, your critical mind would have justified its extreme actions by categorizing you as nuts or at least unstable. Thus from that point forward you would see any similar experiences as being crazy. This reaction would then steer you away from re-experiencing them ever again.

    All our lives can be as pleasing as best sellers. However, this type of AW-based connection is the key. The only variance lies in how well each one person doing the writing understands or fails to correctly interpret and accept what is going on. This understanding directly determines whether an author accepts the experience for what it is or rejects it because of a lack of knowledge. The more one leans toward the later, the slower, more difficult, challenging, less productive and potentially painful the experi-

"I can believe anything, provided it is incredible."
Oscar Wilde

Tom Bird - ~~Write~~ Right From God

ence will be.

To further illustrate this point, allow me to share with a you a story about best selling author Wally Lamb. A few years ago, before making an evening presentation at the University of Missouri in St. Louis, I was hanging out in my hotel room relaxing and doing some channel surfing, when I ran across *The Oprah Winfrey Show*. On this occasion, Oprah was featuring the work of Lamb, who had just authored the best seller *She's Come Undone*.

Oprah, as she always does, prepared extensively for the interview of Lamb backwards and forwards. She also loved Lamb's book, which was why Lamb was on the show in the first place.

Oprah, in her typical enthusiast demeanor, asked Lamb how he had been able to write a book for the layperson on schizophrenia that had hit home so effectively, something that so many others had been trying to do for so long, all of whom had failed miserably. I believe that Oprah was probably looking for some technically laden answer from Lamb about how he had discovered or employed some sort of magic formula to go where no author had ever gone before. Instead, the mild-mannered Lamb surprised even me with the candor and directness of his response.

Lamb simply told the story of how, during one of his routine, daily writing sessions, the image of a woman appeared. Lamb followed his intuition and took some time to explore the background of the woman who sought to communicate very openly with him. As he did that, he gained a greater knowledge until he soon arrived at the point where he trusted her. Once that took place, he literally handed the pen over to the woman and allowed her to write his best seller through him.

His decision, of course, paid off for him, as the book eventually landed on every major national bestseller list in the country. As a result, his fledgling writing career was transformed to one of a best-selling author over night. Now every book that Lamb pens is a best seller even before it's released. All of this came about because he chose to listen to and to give into the experience, which allowed the book to be written for

> Mrs. Bakerman: Dr. Hartley, if you're looking for a new member of our group, I know a nice schizophrenic.
> Mr. Peterson: Or how about a manic-depressive? At least you know they'll be fun half the time.
> The Bob Newhart Show

> "We do not write in order to be understood; we write to understand."
> C. Day Lewis, The Poetic Image

him and through him, and vaulted him to national prominence, which he had obviously been unable to do on his own up to that point.

Wally Lamb was a writer who wanted to be a best-selling author. He tuned to the same exact connection that I have been speaking about and his prayers were answered. This will also work for you, whether becoming an author or not is what you want to do. Understanding enough about how your AW attempts to communicate with you is essential, though, so that you give into the experience and thus allow it to do its work for you.

Your Primary Archetypes Will Do the Writing for You

As you may or may not have already experienced on your own, in one fashion or another, once you give over to a PA, he, she, or it will literally write whatever it is that has been attempting to spring forth from you. When this happens, you will experience a few unique reactions.

First, when whatever it is that you are writing initially begins to come through you, it will have been waiting anxiously for years if not decades. It will also have been used to being an opportunist, ready to take full advantage of whatever situation it can seize, no matter what time or day, you give it to be released.

"If I am rich, it is because I have taken my wages in people. You are my reward."
Quentin Crisp

What this means is that when you first tie into it, it will come flying out at warp speed. It is important during these initial times to keep in deliberate control of your breathing. *If you can control your breathing, you can control your reaction to any situation.* So no matter how you feel, keep breathing deeply. Keep breathing smoothly, through your nose, if at all possible. Make sure to remember to blow out any tension that you may be feeling by taking in as deep of a breath as you can and then exhaling it quickly. It also helps to envision whatever tension it is that you are feeling leaving you at this time in the reflection of a color, shape, or both.

> "Do not put off till tomorrow what can be enjoyed today."
> Josh Billings

Setting a specific time to write each day, as we have already discussed, will immediately and immensely help. Once your AW realizes that you will be providing it with the desired and needed opportunity to release its message each day, it will no longer panic, push you beyond your human limits with an inhuman speed of release, and it will become the compassionate and caring friend that it truly is. It will show up specifically at the time you have designated to begin your writing session and, though reluctantly at first, it will draw each of your writing sessions to a close either at the end of your allotted time frame or immediately after whatever quota of words you may have set for yourself, leaving you with a real emotional and spiritual high before departing.

There also will be no more untimely interruptions by the AW when it senses an opportunity to speak and takes advantage of it by pouring through, like when you are alone driving down the highway and all of a sudden it comes firing through because your critical logical mind has nodded off to sleep. In most cases, of course, not wanting to lose your inspiration you immediately began scrambling for something to write on, or to write with, or both, endangering the lives of all those around you as well as your own. So there will be no more scrambling for pieces of paper, catching inspirations on the back of envelopes or shopping bags. All of this is possible only as long as you continually and consistently make time for your AW, and especially the PAs who it brings with it, as well.

> "I owe my success to having listened respectfully to the very best advice, and then going away and doing the exact opposite."
> G.K. Chesterton

Secondly, when plugged into your AW and its PAs, you will have no idea where it is that you are going on a day-to-day basis. This, like with the first appearance of your unknown or unrecognized PAs, may scare or concern you, all of which is addressed with a blanket solution in the next chapter. Just try to keep control of your reactions during this exciting time, by keeping an eye on your breathing. Remember, if you can control your breathing, you can control your reactions and thus your actions, as well.

Also keep in mind that what you are experiencing is very natural. Please keep in mind that your AW, who may have been waiting on you for decades, wants you to write even more than you may want to. So it will do whatever it has to do to keep you going.

What that means is that your AW will initially offer you only one idea at a time, to keep you from being overburdened. I know, for if you are anything like the typical students who I am so blessed with, that you feel as if your mind is over run with ideas and inspirations. However, the truth is, which I have been able to extract from my extensive experience and research, that even though your present state may appear to bespeak the opposite, your AW offers up only one idea at a time in the early going. The reason that its offerings may appear to be more than one idea is because your AW, as desperate as it had become to grab and capture your attention, will do whatever it can to get you to look its way, even if that means fragmenting the message it is trying to move through you off into several different directions or versions and then tossing then randomly at you like a hungry fisherman dying to catch lunch.

If your AW so desperately wants you to succeed then why does it want to confuse you by not fully exposing the full direction and intent of your work? As I will show in the next chapter, your AW is more than happy to release much finer detail in stages.

The reason that your AW does not release all that you will eventually need to know all at once is because it realizes that if it does so you will lose interest in it and never follow through on the completion of your project, which is very sound logic. Think about it. If you went to a bookstore and purchased a novel, began reading it and twenty-two pages into it you realized exactly how everything was going to turn out, would you be interested in reading through until the end? Of course not. The excitement of discovery would be gone. Thus there would be no reason for you to go on. You would stop there.

Your AW knows you and it knows this about you, as well. So if you only know as much as you need to know to complete that day's writing session, that is good. If you only know enough to complete the next page, paragraph, sentence or word, that's even better. In fact, the less you are consciously aware of, the deep-

"If you limit your choices only to what seems possible or reasonable, you disconnect yourself from what you truly want and all that is left is a compromise."
Robert Fritz

er your connection with your AW, which extends far beyond the confines of your critical/logical mind.

The only way that this situation can work against you is if not understanding scares and thus confuses you. In that case, reread the above section until your reasoning and acceptance becomes crystal clear, and then move on.

How Your PAs Will Introduce Themselves

Following the methods in this excellent book, and performed functionally in the manner that your AW would prefer you to go, normally your top PA, the one carrying the core of your major point, will appear first. There are always exceptions. However, I would say that in over 99% of the thousands of students with which I have dealt, this has been the case. So prevalent is this trend that I believe the only reason that one would vary from this would come as the result of a variance in the procedures laid out in this book.

There are plans which have been given to us to accomplish anything from building a house to becoming an attorney, or a doctor, or a mechanic. For a various number of reasons based on facts and incidents that I have already shared with you, I believe that what I am offering in this book is the Almighty's plan for enabling us to become authors or whatever you want to be in the most productive, yet easy-to-follow, and joyful way possible. Of course, others have taken different routes to their successes. I am not saying that this is the only way. I am saying that this is the fastest and most productive of plans of which I am aware.

Back to your PAs; once your protagonist is fully flushed out, which I will cover how this happens shortly, he, she, or it will then lead you to and introduce you to another PA, who will eventually introduce you to another, who will then introduce his, or her, or itself to you, before leading you to another, and on down the line until all of your PAs have been fully flushed out. The result of this entire experience becomes the understanding you need to trust these PAs to do the work

"Gardens are not made by singing 'Oh how beautiful' and sitting in the shade."
Ruyard Kipling

"The people who get on in this world are the people who get up and look for the circumstances they want, and if they can't find them, make them."
George Bernard Shaw

for you.

Once this has taken place, they will begin meeting during your writing sessions almost as a committee. As discussions are held and decisions are made about the direction and intent of what it is that they will be doing and what role each of them will play in it, and how the specific points that each embodies will be represented. This usually takes place during the *Living Outline* stage. Once that is completed, then whatever you are to write begins taking off on its own and composes itself through your PAs.

A student of mine from Columbus, Ohio, an attorney by trade and a very logical person, was completely astounded by the unfolding of these events as they relayed themselves. Finally, her characters began to commune amongst each other. From that point forward, with each call to me, she would begin with a chuckle and then say, "*well, they decided to...*"

It is not unusual during this stage for your PAs, who definitely have their own minds and destinies, to change their names, their positions in the story or the group, occasionally bring in a new member or to throw out an old one. The entire process functions very much like production meetings leading up to the successful conclusion of a major motion picture. There are always the big ticket actors and actresses and the guiding wisdom of the director. With that, as well, comes much debate and rearranging. That is just how it works in your mind as well as with your PAs.

> "There are no hidden agendas with Tom. He is a real human being. He is what he is and he isn't afraid to share all that he is."
> A Bird Student

> "I am large, I contain multitudes."
> Walt Whitman

Understanding the Backgrounds of Your PAs

Understanding the backgrounds and motivations of your PAs is essential because without this, you will not embody the trust necessary to allow your PAs to do what they, and only they can do, as well as what they must do, which, of course, is to lead you in your writing.

Ponder that for a moment. Before you can trust someone, you first have to know that person. In a personal sense that may mean just getting to know them through dating or hanging out, or whatever the needs of the type of relationship that you have entails. On the business end, you review resumes, call references, interview, and give trial runs on the job. All of this comes as the result of an effort to get to know them and eventually be able to trust the person.

Understanding your PAs so that you will eventually be able to trust them to do their job for you is no different.

The first component that one explores in either a personal or professional association is the sociological background of the person who you are getting to know. You look at where they are from, what kind of family they were raised in, where they went to school, what they majored in, what their parents did for a living, what it is that they most aspire to do with their lives, and what steps they have taken to accomplish these goals, etc., etc., etc. Ultimately, through all of the probing you are looking to answer one question, "*How has this person's past contributed to where he or she presently is in his or her life, and why?*" The last part of that question, featuring the "*why*," is far and away the most important part. It is not enough in your questioning to simply come away with a stock answer. Remember, we seek understandings, which draw us to go beyond mere factual replies, into a much deeper appreciation of the inner workings of our PA's mind, soul, spirit, and life.

After your PAs have offered you all of the necessary stuff you need to understand how where they have come from has contributed to where they are, they will lead you in the direction of coming to grips with their psychological make-ups. In other words, you will be shown "*how what they have experienced in their lives has led them to a specific place in whatever it is that you are writing.*" Your understanding of them in this arena will enable them to take on the fabric that will allow the reader to associate with them on a very deep level. This is also where your PA's motivating passions will come to life.

After your PAs have introduced you to their sociological and psychological backgrounds, they will exhibit for you how these two basic components of their make-ups are reflected on a physical basis in their

> "Strong lives are motivated by dynamic purposes."
> Kenneth Hildebrand

present lives. For example, were we to study the aspects of Herman Melville's legendary character in *Moby Dick,* Captain Ahab, one physical factor of this severely angry man would stand out above the rest. That, of course, would be the man's wooden leg, the result of his last tussle with the great white whale, Moby Dick.

Each time that Ahab enters a scene, his leg continually reminds us of the character's motivating passion, which is his uncontrollable hatred for the whale. The presence of his peg leg is a continual reminder of that throughout the book for us. It also serves as a perfect example of how a character truly represents who he or she is by manifesting it in some form or another physically.

Another good example of this can be drawn from the movie *Rocky*. In the film, Rocky represents an exaggerated version of the "*have nots.*" How is that depicted? It is depicted through Rocky's life itself, where he lives, how he lives, how he dresses, how he talks. You get the idea. What is Rocky's goal? Rocky's goal is to be somebody, to leave all that has been physically manifested in his present life, behind. Of course, in sequels, Rocky does eventually win out enough to be able to leave the physical representations of who he was behind. However, in *Rocky III*, he loses himself after being pummeled by Clubber Lang, played by Mr. T. Then it is only after he returns to his roots that he is able to rediscover his true strength as a fighter and as a man. That is how a PA will represent who he or she represents to you. The physical components of a PA are just tangible representations of the sociological and psychological components that make up each aspect of a PA.

What I have shared with you on how a PA introduces his, her, or itself to you, is simply a system of understanding to better help you get a grasp of what will happen naturally during this stage of your development. If you delve a little closer, you will also see that this represents a very logical understanding, and mimics what we all go through upon meeting a new person or anytime we enter into a new situation.

The first bit of information we always seek con-

> *"Poor is the man whose pleasures depend on the permission of another."*
> Madonna

cerns the sociological background of a person. The next fact we seek to explore has to do with their or its present motivating passion, whether that be an extremely strong like or dislike which is often coupled with questions concerning the physical representation of that in the present.

"So what do you do for a living Bob?"
"You're an accountant."
"How long have you been doing that?"
"Hmmmm, do you like being an accountant?"
"I see. So you really don't like being an accountant, but if you work hard enough it affords you a super opportunity for financial security and early retirement, both of which are your real passions?"

Again, this concept is nothing new to you. In fact, you have been exposed to it thousands of times in your life, from every time you have met someone new, to every time you have watched a movie or read a book.

All that I am attempting to help you do is to take what you presently know so well, that which already comes naturally to you, to your communing with your AW, so you can benefit greatly from that which will be released via your PAs.

"This is above all: to thine own self be true."
William Shakespeare

Who Really are Your PAs?

Who are these PAs, who come to us with their already preformed lives, pasts and motivations? And where do they come from? Those are two questions that persons have been attempting to answer for centuries. Why is it even important that these questions be answered in the first place?

It is important to further our trust and thus our release into the flow of what the AW already has planned for us. After all of my study, experience, and exposure, it is my belief that all writing is autobiographical. If that were true, how then would an individual such as Wally Lamb be able to all of a sudden write a ground breaking book on a topic, such as schizophrenia, that he has never even studied before? It is my belief that this happens because somewhere in Lamb's make-up, background, or experience, he was

"I have a memory like an elephant. In fact, elephants often consult me."
Noel Coward

exposed, first hand, to some sort of schizoid situation. May be it was in a past life, a past love. Maybe he was tapping into and expounding upon the schizoid portion of his own personality or society's strain of it. Either way, or no matter what the situation, it was already there in him, otherwise he would never have been able to tap into it.

That is why, as foreign as it may feel to our logical minds, there is a familiarity with the core topics we are led to write about. It is because somewhere along the way, we were one with it, touched very deeply, even if for only a brief, split second. Either way, it touched us, leaving a tangible imprint on our souls, which we may seek to better understand it and ourselves through reliving some form of the catalyst or experience. Thus we write, and when we write we are writing for ourselves. Anyone who tells you differently is either denying the truth or is a poor writer, because they are too concerned about the feelings of those who would judge them to ever be focused enough on their own. As a result, these persons don't stumble upon their true voices, that which would allow them to truly touch an audience, until they have experienced enough pain from attempting to serve the outside while their insides are starving. Finally, at some time or another though, we all have to go inward. Some of us can only stand doing so for a matter of minutes. As writers, we have to be able to go there and stay there for long periods of time to be able to make the necessary connections with our AWs. Inside, and inside only, is where those connections can be made. And to get there we have to want to get there, which means desiring to do it for one's self.

When at its best and most deep, our writing is autobiographical. This understanding scares us. For we realize that if we are successful in releasing that which is in us, others will know how we really feel, or even more frightening is the fact that we, ourselves will actually know how we feel. That is what truly scares us. For it is then that we will have to face all the unnecessary compromises we have made in our lives, how we have sold out our true selves and how we have imprisoned ourselves as the result of our fears.

"That must be wonderful; I don't understand it at all."
Moliere, 1622

"When the eagles are silent the parrots begin to jabber."
Sir Winston Churchill

So where do PAs come from? They come from somewhere inside of you. Why are they surfacing now? So that your AW can help expose you to them, so that you may understand them and thus grow beyond them, so that you may move farther and faster toward becoming as happy and as productive and vibrant of a reflection of all our potentials, and the Almighty's love, as possible.

Writing becomes the key because it allows us to connect as directly with the Almighty as possible through our AWs. There are other methods available to all of us. Picasso and Michelangelo chose painting, Bergman used films. However, since most of us are not as familiar and thus not as comfortable with painting, sculpting, acting, dancing, and other art forms as we are with writing, which most of us have some exposure to, we chose the latter. That is why you are reading this book now.

"The ancestor of every action is a thought."
Emerson

PA in Non-Fiction

Because so much emphasis has been placed on PAs as characters in fiction up to this point, you may have received the inappropriate impression that the association of Primary Archetypes is pertinent to writing of a fictional nature only. If that be the case, I apologize. For I obviously have not done a fair enough of a job broadening your thinking to fully understand that PAs are the core, the life blood, the trunk of every kind of tree of writing, no matter whether what you write be of a fictional or non-fictional nature.

The biggest distinction between the fictional and non-fictional PAs, is that with the latter there is a greater chance that you will recognize in your PAs the autobiographical portion of you that is attempting to come through in your writing.

For example, a caring math professor who sees life through the equations that he or she knows so well, may have a PA appear in the form of an image of his or herself as a young math student, struggling with certain concepts.

Non-fiction PAs are also usually more recognizable as reflections of our own selves at earlier times in our lives.

To further this point, let me offer up this metaphor. All books are composed of themes. These themes spring from the interactions, expansions and expressions of your PAs. If a PA is expressing freely and thus properly, the trunk of the story grows straight and strong. If the trunk grows straight and strong, the leaves on the tree or its other fruits progress nicely as well, do they not? However, if its roots, as depicted by our PAs, are out of whack, the rest of the tree, all the way out to the leaves or its fruit suffers, as well, thus showing that it all begins with the proper release and understanding of your PAs.

Every book or screenplay is a tree unto itself, which derives its nourishment from the strength of its root system. Non-fiction is no different.

I once had a student who was a professor at a well-known university. This student approached me about her authoring of a textbook in her chosen field of nursing. What made the book so unique in its potential, though, was that it ventured into the uncharted, yet very necessary area of the spiritual components of nursing.

Now this student had done an initial draft of her work which she had retained me to review. When I read the work I was vastly disappointed with the lack of feeling evoked by the work. It was meant to speak to the spirit of her readers but yet it was written in a boring textbook style.

So the first action that I chose to take was to help this student get back in touch with her real self, her AW, the young nurse she once was that had initially led her to her idea, and thus back in touch with those she was attempting to communicate with, as well. After all of the layers of cathartic residue that had hid my student from this reflection of her truer self were removed, she was easily able to re-commune with the truest part of herself that initially had wanted to write this book. It was that vision, that person that became her PA, and it was from that blessed individual's point

---

"Be not simply good; be good for something."
Thoreau

"Great minds have purposes, others have wishes."
Washington Irving

of view that we went back and revised her tale.

The result? After refocusing her project along the lines of her truest, unadulterated calling, via the voice of her PA, the submission package that we were looking for came pouring out of her. A month later, four different publishers had offered her contracts. Uniquely as well, each one of the four commented in their own way that what made her work so special was the fact that it actually spoke to the reader, the young nurses in all of them, and thus it did not read like the typical textbook. The reconnecting of my student to that PA within herself made all the difference. From that realignment in her, sprang an accurate and true depiction of the theme that uniquely drove her. As a result of the full and appropriate release of her theme, the fruits of her labor finally won out.

The same could be said to be true of any successful non-fiction author. When David Halberston wrote his best-selling books on the 40's and 50's, who was he connecting with to write what he wrote? The PA of himself back during those times, and all of the other major influences in his life, and maybe all of our lives, that affected us so greatly.

The enlightening series of books by Joseph Campbell spoke so directly to the reader via the voice of his own PA, which was a reflection of his truest self. Carl Sagan's books, such as *Cosmos*, did the same thing.

Either way, fiction or non-fiction, it all begins with your ability to connect efficiently and consistently with your AW's message, as it is expressed through its ambassadors and voice, your PAs.

> *"If you look good and dress well, you don't need a purpose in life."*
> Robert Pante

A Look Back and a Leap Forward

What you have experienced in your most recent writing exercise was an exposure to both your Transformational and Primary Archetypes. You may want to take a few moments to reflect back upon the latter, which are far less obvious than the TA(s) who greeted you outside the elevator.

However, to make my point crystal clear, I want to conclude this chapter with another exercise sure to bring home to you all that we have already covered.

"I go on working for the same reason that a hen goes on laying eggs."
H.L. Mencken

Step 1. – Take the necessary steps to prepare yourself for this next adventure, and allow your mind to drift back to a very special, maybe even secret or sacred place in your life. Everyone has one. Maybe yours was in your childhood bedroom, in your backyard, in a closet, outside your parent's house somewhere, maybe in a tree. Whatever, allow yourself to go there now, and back to the time when you last went there, and your reason for going there at that time. How was it that you felt at the time? Why were you there? What colors, sounds, temperature surrounded you at the time? Allow them all to come back to life so you can feel as if you were actually back there.

Remember to release any tension you may feel for whatever reason by blowing it out with your breath. Take a few moments just to let yourself go into whatever it was that you felt on that day and at that time.

Step 2. Then allow, out of nowhere, the presence of someone or something, which you have never seen before, to appear along next to you in the image in your mind. Stay with the experience and don't allow your reactions to get the better part of you. Remember to breathe away any and all tension that you may feel. Take as many deep breaths as necessary and blow them out, so that you may become calm and accepting of this experience.

Step 3. Take a few moments to study the image in front of you. What overwhelming feeling or impression do you derive from this person's or this thing's posture or general appearance? Is there a smell that you sense from being around this image or an all-providing feeling?

Turn your focus to the face and then the eyes of this individual. Drink in this person's eyes, until you go beyond these "*windows of the soul*" and directly to the very deepest part of this being. Then, once there, look back out at yourself through the perspective of this individual. From this entity's perspective, what do you see of you? Remember to breathe out any tension that you may be feeling at this time, and don't move onto the next steps until you find yourself perfectly calm and openly responsive.

"I am looking for a lot of men who have an infinite capacity to not know what can't be done."
Henry Ford

Step 4. Allow yourself to drink in any and all reflections of what this person sees and thinks of you. Allow his or her thoughts and feelings to become your own. Then open your eyes and allow all that you feel to be released openly onto the paper before you.

If at any time you lose your connection or your writing comes to a halt before forty-five minutes of time, close your eyes, take a few deep breaths, making sure to reconnect with your nostril breathing, and then connect once again with this individual, and his or her feelings, and begin writing again.

This is also a wonderful opportunity to practice reciprocal communication between you and the images that appear in your mind as the result of your writing. If at any time during this writing exercise or any exercise beyond this point, you have a question of any sort pop up in your mind, in regard to your writing or the AW image produced for you in your mind, don't hesitate to ask of the archetype whatever it is of which you may seek an answer. After you do that, make sure to sit quietly as you await a reply, so that you may receive it through whatever sense you are most accepting of to receive it through.

Chapter Nine:
Let the Cards Do the Trick

"The only thing necessary for the triumph of evil is for good men to do nothing." Edmund Burke

"This is, I think very much the Age of Anxiety." Louis Kronenberger

Back when you were a baby or a very young child, you were openly expressive. If you were happy, you laughed. If you were sad, you cried, and if you were mad, you screamed, yelled, threw something. During those early years, your parents and other family members were your whole world, and they applauded however it was that you felt and whatever form it was that you chose to express it in.

However, as you got bigger and older, much of what was once accepted in you as a young child was no longer seen as acceptable. Over time, we were then taught to think as opposed to feel. The older we got the more this form of living was expected of us. The first step in helping us make what our parents thought to be a necessary conversion, came in the form of being punished, in one way or another, for openly expressing our feelings. Even when we chose to write, we found ourselves trapped behind rules of grammar, punctuation, and spelling.

> "Everyone thinks of changing the world, but no one thinks of changing themselves."
> Tolstoy

The wall or blockage, which I have continually referred to, was constructed from conditioned responses we were expected to make to avoid being punished. It was these knee-jerk responses that eventually took us away from the natural, spontaneous expression of the AW. In essence, it was these conglomerations of conditioned responses, that run cross grain to the open expression of our AW's, that stand between us, our inspirations and the books or screenplays, already written inside of us.

To become one again with this experience, so that the act of expressing can once again become the natural, AW-connected portion of ourselves that it once was, this wall needs to be removed. If it is not removed, you will never be any better, more productive, happier or more successful than you have been up to this point. For each time you choose to follow the callings of your AW, no matter how large or small, you will have to re-climb that ever-heightening wall over and over again to get to that impulse.

In the course of utilizing the suggestions in this chapter, four paramount misunderstandings, Connection Breakers #4, 5, 6, and 7, will be put asunder. Those CBs are:

Connection Breaker Number Four:
Writing is difficult, demanding.

Connection Breaker Number Five:
You should always know what it is that you are writing.

Connection Breaker Number Six:
Not everyone has a major project in them.

Connection Breaker Number Seven:
The past determines the future.

Before we go any further into the aforementioned CBs, let's take a bit of time to understand and realize the brilliance and purpose behind these little but wonderful gems that I affectionately refer to as *"the cards."*

What Are "The Cards" and Why Do They Work?

"Joy is the feeling of grinning inside."
Dr. Melba Colgrove

By cards, I mean 3X5 index cards. My initial introduction to these powerful and useful tools came to me while I was in search of the "absolutes" of writing. During this phase of my development, I was reading every book I could get my hands on that had anything to do with writing. What I was looking for were the steps, or methodology of writing that would enable me to live my dream, which was something that every other profession seemed to have.

While reading through the pile of books that continually surrounded me, I stumbled upon a recently released work by Syd Field, who has gone on to author several other books since on the writing of screenplays, and is far and away the industry's most knowledgeable authority on the subject. In the course of reading his book, Field, an advocate of the "*inside/outside approach to writing,*" suggested that his readers use index cards to release the basic concepts of their screenplays. I began pondering the significance of Field's suggestion and came to the conclusion that this method would also work extremely well with the writing of books. It wasn't long before I put his suggestion into play with my own writing. So effective was his technique, that I have been employing it for the last two decades, not only with my own work, but with that of my students, as well.

When considering why these little gems are so effective and efficient for our use, it is first important to keep in mind that the unconditional AW is both a freedom seeker and a giver of freedom. Thus it does not akin well to any limiting rules and/or restrictions. Instead it prefers pages without lines that will allow it to be itself, to express openly and freely. Index cards provide that option, either by writing on the side without lines or through the purchasing of lineless cards.

Second, it is also absolutely essential to keep in mind that your often exercised critical/logical mind, as opposed to your atrophied AW connected side, is still in control of your consciousness. What that means is that

> "We can secure other people's approval, if we do right and try hard; but our own is worth a hundred of it."
> Mark Twain

your critical/logical mind rides shotgun, monitors your every move, action, thought or decision.

Thank God, though, that the critical mind which is very inflexible, and frankly not very bright, can be fooled or misled very easily. The index cards become very useful in that circumstance because when we begin to release what our AW has to say on them, the condescending and ego controlled critical mind doesn't see us a doing anything of value. All it believes we are doing is scribbling some useless little notes on small scraps of paper. Thus, its authority is not being challenged through the full release of our AW's, and so it feels safe and protected. Typing something on a computer or a typewriter is all out different, of course. In that case, it is not unusual for the critical mind to panic and begin yelling – *"Oh no, she's writing a book! We have to make sure that it's perfect. In fact, we must make sure that it's more than perfect! ... Let's see, do we know enough to write a book? Wait a minute, there's no way that we are bright enough to do this. I mean, who do we think we are, believing that anyone would ever want to read what we had to say?"* And on and on it goes until somewhere along the way you run into some sort of brick wall.

> "Don't take yourself too seriously. And don't be too serious about not taking yourself too seriously."
> Howard Ogden

I'm sure that you understand, having probably been there before already. It is this type of fear that eventually pushes you into closing back up, sometimes for good. However, since writing on index cards doesn't scare your critical mind, because it simply doesn't take you seriously when you work with them, what normally happens via the aforementioned situation will not happen here.

Third, as mentioned, the blockage or wall we seek to remove has been built one conditioned response at a time. Thus to remove this wall, it needs to be taken down one conditioned response at a time. To be able to achieve our ultimate goal during this cathartic stage of our work, each emotion, which is tied to each conditioned response, needs to be identified, acknowledged and expressed individually, given its own voice, and on its own release.

What this translates to in the first of the three stages your work with "the cards" will take, is the expressing of only one thought or idea or image per card, which in most cases translates to only one word. The reason that you are being asked to adhere to this suggestion is because each of the conditioned responses that currently make up the wall between you and your AW need to be given their own voice and opportunity to express what it is that they embody before they can fully be released. It is important to separate these expressions in this way to guarantee that they are given the voice they desire. We do this through the initial stage by limiting ourselves to one thought or feeling or image per card.

> *"When an emotionl injury takes place, the body begins a process as natural as the healing of a physical wound. Let the process happen. Trust that nature will do the healing. Know that the pain will pass and, when it passes, you will be stronger, happier, more sensitive and aware."*
> Peter McWilliams
> *"How to Survive the Loss of a Love"*

How We Will Use the Cards and What They Will Do for Us

The exercise described at the conclusion of this chapter will enable you to utilize "the cards" to take you some place where you have always dreamt of going, but never thought you would ever get to. In general, the index cards will:

1) *Clear away the wall or obstruction that stands between you and your AW;*

2) *Introduce you to your PA's; and*

3) *Release a Living Outline of whatever message, no matter what it happens to be, that has been dying to come out of you for years.*

It is important to keep in mind that all that I am saying will be done naturally as long as you simply:

- *Show up.*
- *Shut up the critical mind via the Three R's of Writing.*
- *Sit Down.*
- *Write.*

> *"Lord make me an instrument of Your Peace. Where there is hatred let me sow love; where there is injury, pardon; where there is doubt, faith; where there is despair, hope; where there is darkness, light; and where there is sadness, joy."*
> *St. Francis of Assisi*

As long as you follow these simple suggestions, you will be giving your AW the chance it needs to break through, and it will take care of the rest through its work with the index cards. Remember, these four steps are all you need to be responsible for. If you follow them consistently all that you have wanted to do as a writer and as a person will magically appear before your eyes, such as in the cases listed below.

Phase One – The Cathartic Cleansing

This is the first stage of what will happen to you as you begin your work with "the cards" through the exercise at the conclusion of this chapter.

Remember, this will happen naturally and on its own as long as you follow the *Three R's of Writing* from the previous chapter on a daily basis. It is also important to keep in mind during this phase to release only one thought, feeling, or image onto each card, which in most cases translates to one word.

You will be somewhat surprised, if not shocked, when you begin using "the cards" and entering into this phase. For thoughts and feelings, most of which you will have denied for years if not decades, will begin to express themselves. Since these cathartic expressions will have absolutely nothing to do with whatever it is that you may have felt that you wanted to write, you will initially wonder what is going on. Thoughts, feelings and images of fears, frustrations, and angers in general will begin flying out of you like poop out of a goose. This phase signals the AW's dropping down off the wall that exists between you and it. Please be aware that if you fully give into this process this one time and keep writing in one shape or another from this point forward, this catharsis will never have to be repeated ever again. Your AW will see to that as long as it is given a forum for unadulterated expression on a consistent basis. The result of this phase is that your AW is once again freed back into your life, and you will never go back to being frightened or over compromised ever again.

> *Quit now, you'll never make it. If you disregard this advice, you'll be halfway there.*
> *David Zucker*

Testimonial

Following is a student of mine, Sharon Newman, and her first-hand account of this unique step.

Sharon Newman:
Week One of Working with Her Cards

"Well, well, well. The things one learns about one's self. A psychologist would probably say I have real problems when it comes to dealing with my emotions. After reviewing "the cards", I would have to say that I agree. While there were emotions of sadness and anger expressed, there wasn't any sense of 'me' in "the cards". I'm mot really sure that I understand or can explain what I mean by that, but I'll try.

"I like to think of myself as being open to new experiences, but writing down my feeling put me off. I know there is more to life than pain and rage. If there weren't, I would have probably died of a heart attack by now.

"I feel joy and other emotions as a result of writing, but "the cards" clearly show that I've bottled up every emotion inside of me except the two which society deems acceptable to show. We aren't supposed to show emotions. We're supposed to be like robots, never losing our control or grips over ourselves. I've cultivated that reputation for myself at work and it has carried over into all aspects of my life.

"No one really knows the depth of my pain or how much I feel like a child when I play games. Only when I am alone and the door is shut and the room is dark so all the feelings of isolation, loss, and grieving hit me.

"Oh and there are those times when I'm driving my car and that certain country ballad comes on, and I cry for what I've lost even if the song is happy. I've forgotten what happiness and joy feel like. I've forgotten what it means to feel peace and contentment. The truth is that I've totally lost touch with my feelings and with those around me.

"It hurts too much to let any of those feelings

creep in. To be honest with you. I hated this assignment the first day. It completely put me on edge. It felt like a chore I 'had' to do. All the self defeatist attitudes showed up. The only feeling I have is one of rage because it is the safest for me to feel right now.

"The irony of the situation is this outline is going well but that spark of emotion that lifts a story from being mere words to being real is missing. I see it and feel it. I am very passionate about my book, but it doesn't have that stomach churning conflict. It's just another story that anyone could write.

"I am just so very resistant to feeling. I have to get through the block so my characters can fully live. I just don't know how to do it."

"But if a man happens to find himself he has a mansion which he can inhabit with dignity all the days of his life."
James Michener

Sharon Newman:
Week Two

"Sometimes I find it totally amazing what a little time and perspective can do for a person – me specifically. This is the second week I am writing on my reaction to what I call my 'emotion cards'. To be completely honest I didn't have a very good (easy) first week but I did notice a shift this week.

"I feel that my anger and pain are slowly easing their way out of "the cards". I don't feel so dominated by those two feelings any more.

"Several times throughout "the cards" I found myself asking my permission to let me feel. It sounded crazy to me when I started but it doesn't feel weird to me now. In fact, it makes perfect sense. I had closed myself off so tightly from the emotions of others around me and what I personally felt, that I had to give myself the chance to decide if I wanted to feel again. 'Inevitable' is the only word I can use to describe how I felt when I made my choice. The resistance to feeling is still in the core of my inner self but I'm not totally resistant any longer.

"Paradise is where I am."
Voltaire

"At times I feel like I've opened myself to the 'me' that I had never seen before. There are feelings I never even knew existed. I remember at one point in "the cards" I was learning things about myself I never would consciously allow to enter my mind. The feelings were not pleasant, and it seemed to hurt me physically, but I got through it all with a box of Puffs.

"When the session was over I felt stunned at what I had found. The fact was I feared what was in my heart. I revealed my secrets and lived through the experience. I didn't crack in two and I felt that fear no longer had a hand on my throat.

"Every day I look at the brick wall I've built for myself and I imagine the more I let myself feel, the more the bricks crumble to the ground, leaving a beautiful view of the sky. The first week I knocked one brick out of place, and the second week I'm on the fifth and sixth blocks.

"I feel good about what I've accomplished. To me, what I have done is important. Getting the chance to validate my own feelings made me feel like I am necessary and have a purpose in this world.

"One of the important keys I found for myself came when I accepted the negative or 'bad side' of myself. From that point forward I found it a whole lot easier to be good to myself. "The cards" reflected my need to be free. I want positive feelings and events to come into my life. For the first time in a long while. I really want to be good to me.

"I feel hope and positive emotions at war with my darker side. I've discovered a confidence in myself I suspected was there.

"I want desperately to win this fight with myself. There is still resistance in me, and it takes real effort to beat down that hurdle every day. It's not easy and I don't always win, but at least now both sides are equally armed and no one wins all the time.

"I don't dread "the cards" like I did the first week. In fact, I look forward to getting out how I feel.

"If there is a downside to this process of feeling for me it would be the infusion of feelings where I work. I prefer to keep my feelings and attitudes to myself when I'm there. But lately the emotional side has been peeking through at odd times when my self-control is slightly relaxed. The fact that people are now beginning to see how I feel still bothers me some, but not too much. It's a small price to pay to allow feel-

Beyond plants are animals, beyond animals is man, beyond man is the universe, the Big Light, let the Big Light in!
Jean Toomer

ings like happiness and joy into my life for the first time in years.

"I feel like I'm moving forward to the place I want to be. I realize that it will be a long time until I get there, but I am on my way.

"The credit for my push forward goes to two places. The first is the emotion cards and your suggestion to use them. Secondly, I feel I deserve some of the credit. Not only did I fulfill the assignment, but I also learned about myself and my feelings in the process. This idea of taking pride in myself feels weird but right.

"I am ready."

MAE WEST: For a long time I was ashamed of the way I lived.
"Did you reform?"
MAE WEST: No; I'm not ashamed anymore.

Phase Two – Hello PA's

As the wall between you and your AW falls, the necessary space will be for whatever it is that seeks to write itself through you to begin expressing itself through your PA's. Contrary to the cathartic phase, you can write as much as you want on each card. You no longer have to limit yourself to one thought or feeling or image per card.

In each case your PA's will eventually, totally, and completely appear as an image. In some cases this image will be personified in the form of a human or an animal. In other cases, especially pertaining to non-fiction, your images will manifest in the form of strategic depictions of how the themes that will make up your work can and will be best expressed.

In either case, these images will continue to evolve and introduce themselves to you on "the cards" until all have been released and fully fleshed out right before your eyes, so that you may derive the proper understandings and thus confidence to embrace the next phase.

Testimonial

Following is a another student of mine, Angelyn Bales, and her first hand account of this step.

Angelyn Bales:
What it Felt Like to Work on the Index Cards During the First Few Weeks

"She got even in a way that was almost cruel. She forgave them.
Ralph McGill on Eleanor Roosevelt

"I remember that Tom and I talked on the phone on a Friday afternoon, and he gave me my first assignment which was to write 100 index cards a day for the next ten days. After those ten days I was asked to spend the next three days just relaxing and sorting "the cards" into piles I thought would go together. Later that evening, I went to a local drugstore to do some household shopping and bought a stack of index cards.

"When I got home I thought about doing "the cards" and became more and more enthusiastic about starting on them. I unwrapped "the cards", sat down on the floor in my living room, and started writing whatever came to my mind.

"Tom said that I could put anything on "the cards" that pertained to the novel I wanted to write – I could put one word per card if I wanted. So for the first few days I wrote one words on each card. It was fun, and I was excited about the whole process. I had so many ideas in my head related to the novel and really needed a place to put them. "The cards" provided a way for me to do that – sort of like a container to put my ideas and feelings into so that I could keep them and look back at them. The words that I put on "the cards" came to mind very easily, so it felt like a good beginning. I was finally doing something about my desire to write a novel.

"By perseverance the snail reached the ark."
Charles Haddon Spurgeon

"During the first week I worked on "the cards" in the early evening. I would sit on the floor and just let the words come out. It was a pleasant experience, and I felt like I was accomplishing something. As time went by, it became more difficult for me to think of things to write on "the cards". By the seventh or

> "If error is corrected whenever it is recognized as such, the path of error is the path of truth."
> Hans Reichenbach

> "There is no good, in arguing with the inevitable. The only argument available with an east wind is to put on your overcoat."
> James Russell Lowell

eighth day I had to dig deeper into myself in order to put ideas and feelings down.

"There was one day when I was so physically tired in the evening that I didn't do "the cards" at all - I had to do twice as many the next day. That's when I realized that the evening wasn't the best time for me to work on "the cards". I switched to doing them in the mornings; it was difficult to switch the schedule I had already set for myself. Eventually, I got used to my new schedule and it has worked out better because I'm more energetic.

"Writing "the cards" usually happened quickly. Sometimes I could write 100 cards in thirty minutes sometimes it would take an hour. After I finished the first ten days of cards and started sorting them, the sorting happened quickly, also. It took a couple of hours. I remember them going into piles automatically.

"I put little labels down in front of the piles: character description, plot, feelings about story, ideas for story, and so on. The whole process defined itself – I didn't have to think about it very much. Afterwards, I wrote about my feelings and ideas that came out in the process of doing the assignment. I was surprised that I was able to write so much. I thought, '*Wow, this really is an incredible task - I mean it seems so simple and sounds so simple, but it really helps to get these ideas and feelings out and bring them up to the surface.*' I felt like I was shaking my whole body, being and soul. It was satisfying and fulfilling.

"Writing this novel was something I'd wanted to do for many years. I thought, '*I'm finally doing this.*' It was a breakthrough for me, so that's the exhilaration. On the other hand, I was afraid to begin the process. I was terrified of the unknown. I thought I might fail or my work wouldn't be good enough or people wouldn't like it. It felt satisfying to have something down on paper and to have a feel for where I was headed. I thought '*Yes, I really can do this*'.

"I became so aware of myself and how important writing was to me. I thought how fortunate I was to have someone who knows what he's doing to guide me through these steps. I'm the kind of person who tends to look at the final product and feel overwhelmed.

Then I get stuck in the process because I don't focus on each step leading to the result. I keep looking at the end product and thinking about how much work it will take to produce it. It was really helpful to have someone break the writing process down into steps. That was exactly what I needed - to focus on the step and the daily experience of writing.

"Tom suggested that I relax on the day we have our telephone meetings – it's always a Wednesday morning - he told me not write anything on those days, just celebrate what I had done during the past week. He suggested that I do something fun, and I liked the idea. For years on Wednesdays, I've been having lunch with a friend who is a painter. Now I get to tell her about my writing experiences of being an artist. It's helpful to talk to another person who understands the process of working on a creative project.

"The second assignment was to write 200 cards a day for five days, and on the sixth day to sort "the cards" into piles. Then, I was to write down how I felt. What happened with the second assignment turned out to be emotionally difficult.

"The imagination may be compared to Adam's dream –he awoke and found it truth."
Keats

"The first day I worked on "the cards" I felt very sad, low in confidence, and had a fear of failure. The second day I had more of those same feelings and additionally, I felt like I was at loose ends - like I was falling apart. I felt tired because those emotions were overwhelming me. There were times when I worked on "the cards" that I felt like I couldn't do any more of them. I was tired and drained. I didn't have any more ideas. I had a huge range of emotions.

"On the third day, I began to feel stronger, not so sad and fearful. I felt like my emotions were turning toward the positive. I didn't feel quite so tired. On the fourth day, I felt more and more confident. I thought, '*Yes, I can do this. I can write this story.*' On the fifth day, I started believing in the entire process – I mean really believing and letting go of some fear - just relaxing and realizing that I needed to be open and let go of the perfectionist tendencies. If I would do those things, the process would happen. I likened it to my horseback riding. Sometimes I try too hard to be precise in my technique and to be in control. What I've learned is

"When love and skill work together, expect a masterpiece."
John Ruskin

that when I let go of all those worries and let my body relax and do what I know how to do, then I'm more in sync with the horse and it really works. Then it becomes a flow experience.

"On the sixth day, when I began sorting "the cards" for the second assignment, I noticed that a lot of what "the cards" contained were words depicting my range of emotions: *'despondent,' 'terrified,' 'exuberant,'* and *'joyful'*. Some of "the cards" were about the plot and characters. However, I had to focus on my array of emotions before I could focus on the story itself. Honestly, it was difficult to go through the week. I felt like I had turned inside out, like I was being deconstructed and reconstructed. I went from feeling very sad, scared, and at loose ends to feeling stronger, confident, and calm. Something inside me had shifted and reorganized. Maybe it was my emotional energy, or the energy that was going into all those different emotions got shifted and re-channeled in a more positive direction.

"Talking to Tom on the seventh day was cathartic. I described my feelings to him, and he replied that there is a cathartic process that takes place. He said the process would continue, but it would lessen in intensity as time went by. That experience was a difficult one, emotionally and physically. Tom reminded me that writing a book was something I wanted to do for many years, and for different reason I hadn't started it until that point in time. So I was letting go of familiar habits and pieces of myself, and that's hard to do. I felt sadness at letting go of a part of myself and heading in a new direction that's uncertain.

"Another interesting thing happened during that week of the second assignment: I became physically ill. I felt like I had a bad cold or the flu. I began to feel badly on the first day. By the fourth day I had a number of flu-like symptoms. On the fifth day I went horseback riding, even though I felt tired because I had a lesson I couldn't miss. I rode better than I had in months. I believe in the midst of "coughing up" all those feelings and letting them go my riding was affected. That day I felt more in sync with the horse than ever before. I didn't have to think about what I

And God smiled again, and the rainbow appeared, and curled itself around his shoulder.
James Weldon Johnson

It is not enough to have a good mind, The main thing is to use it well.
Rene Descartes
1637

was doing – I just let it happen. It was a breakthrough for me in my riding. I believe some sort of breakthrough happened in my writing as well. The next day I began to feel better physically."

Phase Three – The Living Outline

"He who has a why to live can bear almost any how."
Nietzsche

As your PA's step fully into your consciousness, bright, clear images of what it is that they will be writing with you will pop into your mind, until all of your writing on "the cards" becomes devoted to the relaying of what lies inside you. As with Phase Two, write as much per card as you would like.

Some of what will be released in this phase will astound you as the message you have been carrying around with you, with the cathartic wall now removed, begins to be released in outline form into your consciousness.

What a confidence builder that is to finally be introduced to the message or purpose that has been driving you all these years, and to know, without a doubt, that there is a major project such as this actually living inside you. Along these same lines, much of what you have received glimpses of over the years will finally begin to make sense as the pieces of this puzzle are finally given the opportunity to fall into place.

"It is the supreme act of the teacher to awaken joy in creative expression and knowledge."
Albert Einstein

The whole idea behind this phase is to keep releasing whatever it is that has been trying to get out of you onto "the cards" until you no longer have anything new to say.

Beyond Phase Three

At that point, stop writing on "the cards", and go out and purchase the largest bulletin board that you can find and a few hundred tacks to go along with it.

Once you have done that, take the time you had designated to work with your cards each day, follow the preparatory steps to insure you are in an AW connected state, and being sorting your cards into three distinct sections:

1) *Cathartic Material.*
2) *Releasing of PA's.*
3) *Your Living Outline.*

Set "the cards" for the first two sections aside and take the remaining cards for the *Living Outline* and begin tacking them in chronological order on your bulletin board. If you have so many cards that they don't all fit on one bulletin board, you may need to consolidate some of your comments down from several cards to one or two.

Once you have allowed your *Living Outline* to come to life, use your writing time each day to reflect upon the composition or arrangement of your *Living Outline*. Continue to utilize your index cards for this purpose. After entering into your AW connected state, gaze up at your bulletin board and allow anything you feel to be captured on separate index cards. At the conclusion of each days session, sort the newly composed expressions into one of the three aforementioned categories, and group them with "the cards" you have already written. In regard to any new insights that may have appeared on your *Living Outline*, tack them up on your bulletin board in the appropriate locale. Continue to do this until nothing new comes to you in response to your *Living Outline*, and all that you have to say has been reflected.

"Here is the test to find whether your mission on earth is finished: If you're alive, it isn't." Richard Bach

The CBs That #4, 5, 6 and 7 Disproves

Connection Breaker Number Four:
Writing is Difficult, Demanding.

The former is definitely true if one chooses not to grow beyond the wall of the inappropriate beliefs and conditionings that we have spoken about, and removed through our use of "the cards". For without first removing all of the doubt and criticism that can get in your way, every step forward feels like you are lifting the entire weight of the entire world along with you. However, if you severely lighten that load by ridding yourself of the unnecessary bulk and baggage of the aforementioned, you will feel as light as a feather as you dance down the road toward the successful release of your message.

Connection Breaker Number Five:
You Should Always Know What You Are Writing.

> *"Unhappiness is in not knowing what we want and killing ourselves to get it."*
> Don Herold

Let's attack this one from a purely human perspective. If you always knew where it was that your reading was going and how it was going to end, would you need to, and thus have any desire to, finish it? Of course not. There would be no reason to.

The same goes with writing. It is natural, normal, typical, all of the above, for you to not know where it is that you are going or oftentimes what it is that you are writing about when you are approaching it correctly. The reason for this is that your AW exists beyond the vision of your critical/logical mind. Thus, it is only normal that when you are in touch with your AW that your critical/logical mind in no way can decipher or accurately anticipate what it is which it has to share or say. Also, since your AW speaks in such a vastly different way and tone and about much broader, more universal themes, there is no way that the critical/logical mind could in any way even come close to either understanding or correctly anticipating the result of your AW connected writing. In fact, one of the ways in which I know that my students are properly connected to their AW's, is that they have no idea where it is that they are going. They write like they read, seeking resolution and understanding in regard to what lies around the next bend. Then, and only then, are they in the correct place and space.

> *"My choice early in life was either to be a piano player in a whorehouse or a politician. And to tell the truth, there's hardly any difference."*
> Harry S. Truman

Initially, of course, most of those using this system for the first time, are shocked and confused by this experience; or at least their logical, critical minds are. So many enter into my seminars, workshops, and

> "Our memories are card indexes consulted, and then put back in disorder by authorities who we do not control."
> Cyril Connolly

> "When one door of happiness closes, another opens, but often we look so long at the closed door that we do not see the one that has been opened for us."
> Helen Keller

retreats believing that they want to write this or that. However, I instantly recognize that their mere presence in my class tells me than they are disconnected in one way or another from what it is that is truly trying to be released from them. For if they were properly aligned with their AW's, and had become one with that all empowering connection, they wouldn't need my offerings in the first place, because they would already be leading the lives that they sought. With their writing, if they were properly tied into their AW's, their books and screenplays would be streaming uncontrollably through them and they wouldn't have time for mine or any other course. They would be devoting every available minute to the functional release of their inspirations.

To help verify this, one of the first questions I ask of them is: "*how long each one of them has wanted to write?*" The average length of time is approximately twenty years, which tells me a tremendous amount about the make-up of each class as well.

First, their responses tell me that there was something, an event, an inspiration, a loss, an awakening that at one time or another caused a strong enough of an emotional reaction on each of their ends that some sort of breakthrough was made with their AW's. When this occurred, their AW's were then able to pass through a large amount, but far from all, of the background and description of what it was that was waiting to be written through each one.

Once this information was transferred, it landed in the realms of their individual consciousnesses, which is of course controlled by the critical/logical mind, who now had to come up with an explanation and rationalization for the inspirations released by the AW. Ah, here is where the big mistake is made, which also forms the foundation for all of our miscues through the years – for the vastly limited capabilities of the critical/logical mind are put in charge of the enlightened output of the AW.

Because of its limited scope, the critical/logical mind doesn't understand the AW based expression, so it fears it. As the result of fearing it, the critical/logical mind then attempts to destroy it by homogenizing that which makes it so different. In doing that, of course, it zaps the life, zest and thus the heart and universal appeal from it until it becomes something, safe, logical, achievable – controllable. Over time, the critical/logical mind reduces wide reaching, universal ideas to the children's books that most grade school teachers enter into my classes believing that they want to write, only to discover that once the AW is released that it is a mainstream novel or screenplay that they really want to pen. As they leave the class, they feel enlightened, in touch with their true selves, even they have no idea where it is that their AW related ideas are going, or how they are ever going to write it.

"Our doubts are traitors, and make us lose the good we oft night win by fearing to attempt." William Shakespeare

Second, all of this, of course, comes as the result of being AW connected, which the *Three R's of Writing* do for you. The Cards tear down the wall between you and your AW so that this transition can become permanent in your writing, and in your life as well.

When you are then connected to your AW, words will begin to flow out of you that you had no conscious idea where they were going, and/or you will find yourself writing passionately, expressively and confidently about topics your logical mind tells you that you are not qualified to write. Or it tells you that you are not old enough, young enough, educated enough or whatever. It is then that you are in the correct place, space and mode, for only than are you AW connected, which is where you need to be to be effective in any way, shape, or form as an author.

Connection Breaker Number Six:
Not Everyone Has A Major Project In Them.

I believe this statement to be partially true. No, I do not believe that everyone has a major project in them. Instead, I believe that some persons choose other forms of deep communication, whether it be painting, acting, sculpting or whatever, to express the universal callings of their souls. However, I do believe that everyone that wants to write wants to do so because at one time or another, maybe even before they came to this place, these individuals chose writing as their form of expression for conveying and leaving behind, the special message which they embody.

First, these persons write for themselves so that their critical/logical minds can understand and then embrace who they really are. Then once it is available in book form, it is also available for their use with others. However, whether their book or screenplay sells to or affects millions or no one outside themselves, it will have still served a huge purpose by severely bettering their own lives, which can only be good for all of us as well, since at one level or another, we are all interconnected.

How do I know this to be true? Because over nearly the last twenty years, I can honestly say that I have not had a person come to me that felt the urge to write, who, when the proper steps were taken, did not have a book begin to come out of them. Because of what was just alluded to in my breaking down of CB# 6, most of that which came out of them was different if not vastly different from what they had expected, but that is the norm when dealing with the AW.

The major criticism against this train of thought stems from the belief that writers are special people born with a special purpose, message and/or story inside them. Your work with "the cards" will show you that you are one of those special persons, as the walls between you and your AW are removed and the book or screenplay that has been trying to get out of you for possibly decades comes flowing through in the form of your *Living Outline*. It is also at this time, when your own personal blinders that have kept you from seeing your true self, and the true brilliance of others around you as well, that you will discover that we are all special persons with special messages, and that writers are simply those persons who have chosen the art form of writing, for whatever reason, to convey it.

"Courage is doing what you're afraid to do. There can be no courage unless you're scared."
Eddie Rickenbacker

Connection Breaker Number Seven:
The Past Determines the Future.

If that's the truth, then we're all screwed. For if we believe in CB# 7, then we have to believe that we can never learn, never grow and thus never change – all of which is absolutely ridiculous, of course. We are learning, growing, and changing every day.

This excuse has served your critical/logical mind well over the years though, for it has caused you to believe that there was no real use in you trying any way. Because, either way, nothing was ever going to change. So why even try something different if you were just going to remain the same struggling, failure of a writer anyway?

The truth is that no matter now much energy, effort or time that you may have placed into your writing up to this time, if you were driving down the wrong road, there was still no chance at all that you were going to get to where you wanted to go. Where you long to go is, of course, where your true self, your AW has been calling you to go.

Following the *Three R's of Writing*, puts you back on the road. Using "the cards" widens that road from a path to a super highway, and the rapid direction that you will be traveling in from that point forward will reap huge changes. Your writing will become magical and your words and your life will come alive – instantly.

"To see a world in a grain of sand and heaven in a wild flower, to hold infinity in the palm of your hand and eternity in an hour."
William Blake

Putting "The Cards" into Play

I recently saw a greeting card at a local store that really grabbed my attention. On the outside cover was a three stage photo of a young, white dove, first jumping off a limb, then opening its wings and then taking flight. The inscription on the inside of the card simply read: "Sometimes all that is needed is a leap of faith." So true with just about any experience, especially this one. That is all you will need here, as well, the writing, "the cards" and your AW will take care of the rest. What will happen as a result of this experience is that:

1) *The wall between you and your AW will be permanently removed;*

2) *You will reconnect or connect with your AW serving PA's for the first time, who will;*

3) *Release a blueprint version of that which has been causing you to want to write for so long, via your Living Outline.*

All of which will:

1) *Enable you to reconnect with your real self and your AW;*

2) *Finally give you the confidence, connection and insight to properly commit to that which you have felt drawn to for so long;*

3) *Form the foundation of whatever it is your living message may be.*

4) *To successfully complete this step, you will need to purchase a minimum of 1,500 3X5 index cards. The Cards which are unlined on both sides would be the best. However, if all you can find are those which are lined on one side, simply use the unlined side when writing with this drill.*

As mentioned, if you can arrange your schedule to write first thing after awakening to the day, that would be most productive for you and thus in your best interest. This experience will only take between one and three weeks to complete. If you do fall outside the lines of the following daily routine, this experience will end up taking you far longer to complete. The reason for that is that the proper application of consistency is essential in the changing of any habit or thought form. If you are able to apply yourself to this on a daily basis, the insecurities and inappropriate thought patterns that you are tearing down will never have a chance to regroup and counterattack. The best defense is always a good offense. Thus you will never have to deal with the same distractions twice. You can just keep leaping forward from release to release, from revelation to revelation, until the pathway for your PA(s) has been cleared, and then they can release your

"Even if you're on the right track, you'll get run over if you just sit there."
Will Rogers

"When you get right down to the root of the meaning of the word "succeed," you find it simply means to follow through."
F. W. Nichol

Living Outline, freeing you to see not only what is inside of you, but allowing you the confidence that can come only as a result of experiencing what your purpose is, as well. From that point forward, commitment and consistency will come much easier as you and the project and your AW begin to function as one.

The hour that you initially set aside may seem like a great stretch for you, but that feeling only comes as the result of your critical/logical mind's rejection of the entire idea, because it feels its authority over your life is being challenged. Don't worry though. This will all subside quickly in a day or two after the positively addictive tendencies of writing take over. This happens, of course, because of the emotional high you will receive as the result of the unconditional love that will come streaming through after the cathartic phase. Once that high hits, and the unconditional connection and love grabs a hold of you, you will have a much more difficult time walking away from your writing than you will walking towards it. So what I am saying is that all you have to do is to make it beyond the cathartic phase and you will be on autopilot.

As mentioned earlier in this chapter, you will go through three phases of development and release your work with your cards. This will happen naturally and all on its own as long as you simply show up, shut up, sit down and write. Your AW will take care of the rest.

To best facilitate this step, follow the procedures that I have already conveyed to help you relax and then reach the desired AW connection. The more nervous or uneasy you are to take this step, the more your critical/logical mind is reacting and the riper you are for this experience. Since this step is exhilarating and extensive, suggestions and mile markers for interpreting and fine-tuning your efforts will be dropped in at the conclusion of the following chapters, and no extra writing exercises will be added in.

Begin this step as soon as possible. By waiting longer than one day you will only be adding to the pile of cathartic material that you are already responsible for taking care of.

Start now or as soon as possible. Your PAs, and most of all the ecstasy you long to feel, that can only

> "Only the curious will learn and only the resolute overcome the obstacles of learning. The quest quotient has always excited me more than the intelligence quotient."
> Eugene S. Wilson

> "We must cultivate our garden."
> Voltaire

come through your connection with your AW, awaits you.

Chapter Ten:
Consistently Reinforce Your
AW Dreams and What It Releases
Through You

"Whether you think you can, or that you can't, you are usually right."
Henry Ford

Up until this point in your life, just about everything around you has told you not to feel, not to write; so much so that the effect of those few persons or situations that did the opposite were easily disavowed and swallowed up. Let's examine this predicament from a closer perspective.

It all began with your family, your community and your friends expecting you to fall in line. Why you did, when you walked that safe route there in the middle, you were accepted, rewarded, appreciated. When you did not, you were treated just the opposite and you were punished, made fun of or, ignored, criticized, yelled at. Then you stepped into the educational arena, which, of course, was created by, and thus was an extension of, those influences who had done their darnest to save you from yourself. Of course, the rules got a lot sterner and the punishments much more severe, and less caring and understanding as you got older, as your zest for freedom and expression expanded. Some sort of organized religious element may have been sprinkled in just for effect. The purpose of this was to first inform you and then convince you of the fact that there was only one God – theirs – and only one way to He, She, or It, and that was, of course, through their way. What that all boiled down to, on all levels that could potentially affect your life, was that if you were one of them, you were good, sane and saved. If you weren't, well....God rest your soul.

"The question is not what you look at, but what you see."
Henry David Thoreau, 1830

This bombardment of influence hitting you from all directions, forced you away from your AW, who fell not within the lines of man's rules. For He, She, or It knew a better way and thus chose to live outside of all the rules and regulations. But in following the ways of your AW, you were bound to lose all of those persons around you, all of whom supposedly cared for you.

Now you have reached a stage or time in your life when all that on the outside is not nearly as important as that which calls to you from the inside. For that which calls to you from the inside has never deserted you and has been with you since birth. That which calls to you is, of course, your AW. Whether you arrived at this point as the result of a desire, desperation, an awakening, out of fear that you would never have all that your soul desires and thus you may never be all that you could and want to be if you don't act now, doesn't matter. All that does matter is that you are here now, and ready, willing, and prepared to take this all important step.

"I can't tell a lie - not even when I hear one."
John Kendrick Bangs

The Simple Truth

The simple truth is that all you have been exposed to up to this point, all the less than productive thinking and conditional circumstances you have accepted, have had a distinct effect on you. The sheer repetition of these influences have caused you to associate pleasure with the denial of your AW, and pain associated with anything having to do with writing.

We don't have to look back very far to be slapped in the face by this sort of influence. Just consider how writers are depicted in movies or in books. Is there ever a sane one? No, all are either broke, crazy, or under intense pressure to meet an impossible deadline. A victory for them is seen as somehow miraculously not having to be buried in a common grave, of having the rare and unique pleasure of actually seeing a bit of fame and reward before their drug habit or some grotesque sexually transmitted disease prematurely ends their pitiful lives. Of course, this form of erroneous characterization has made for wonderful copy for centuries. But it has done tremendous damage to our willingness and ability to connect with, or even want to consider connecting with our AW's. The truth, of course, is all around us. Persons such as best-selling author John Grisham were able to break through all of the dogma and succeed not only financially but retain their personal virtues, as well. All you have to do is to look beyond what you have been told and the truth speaks for itself.

Grisham was a struggling attorney, with no formal training in writing before listening to his AW paid off in hundreds of millions of sales that led him to become the literary voice of America. What wasn't Stephen King before the following of his inner voice - that AW-based connection we all have - led him away from his jobs as a janitor, a convenience store clerk and onto the best seller list for the last twenty years plus. Andrew Greeley was a priest. Tom Clancy was in insurance. Anthony Robbins was too young and didn't even have a real job yet. In fact, very rarely do you find a successful author who is a direct byproduct of the societal and educational system which has unknowingly strived so hard to steer us away from our true selves. In one way or another even Ph.D.s and others have had to step outside the system to find themselves and to connect with their true purposes.

"The most difficult persons that I have to work with are those with Ph.D.s," claims New York Editor Michael Seidman. *"They focus way too much on the*

> *"The only true happiness comes from squandering ourselves for a purpose."*
> William Cowper

> *"Don't try to take on a new personality; it doesn't work."*
> Richard Nixon

rules, instead of the heart and how the rules can work for the heart."

Outside the literary arena and into the personal realm, the inappropriate influences are just as rampant. How many times have you been applauded in the past when compared to the number of occasions when you have either received a patronizing or down right critical response to your desire to write?

"First time authors can't get published."

"But why would you want to write Honey? You have that nice job down at the bank."

"Why don't you just join a book reading group or maybe take a class in creative writing or something to cure this ridiculous urge of yours? You're no writer honey. You're a housewife and you have children and Bob to take care of. Isn't that enough? Why would you even want to write a book and risk losing all that?"

"What you wrote was really nice, and I'm really proud of you for doing so well. But you're so young. I just don't think that anyone is really going to take you seriously. Plus, I don't really think there is a future in it. Why don't you put that wonderful mind of yours to work in something with a better future associated with it? Something like accounting, or law, or medicine, do you know what I mean? Then when you've gotten your degrees and you have a little spare time you can take it up as a hobby."

"What? Write a book at your age? You have to be kidding? It takes forever to get something written and published, and there may not be that much time left. Plus, whose really going to want to hear what you want to write about anyway? Why not put your time to better use? Travel, take up a hobby, spend more time with the grandkids?"

"You want to do what? You want to write books? But how are you going to make a living?"

The last one especially gets to me. Do you know that I have been authoring books for nearly two decades now, and yet when people first meet me they still say to me – "Ah, so you write books; how do you make a living then?" The odd circumstance about all of this is that in the vast majority of cases, the AW connected activities that they have run away from, and to

> "A little less hypocrisy and a little more tolerance toward oneself can only have good results in respect for our neighbor; for we are all too prone to transfer to our fellows the injustice and violence we inflict upon our own natures."
> Carl Jung

which I have directed my life have brought so much more to my life, including financial gain, then they have yet to experience in theirs.

How they react, though, is not their fault. They, like you, in one degree or another, have just been taught to associate writing with deprivation and pain. Even though the evidence contrary to that is all around them, they cannot see it because of how they have been conditioned to see and then react. This string of conditioned knee jerk-responses is also what has held you back from pouring yourself into a writing profession or into any endeavor dealing with your writing, and now it's time to change all that.

> *"What seems nasty, painful, evil, can become a source of beauty, joy and strength, if faced with an open mind. Every moment is a golden one for him who has the vision to recognize it as such."*
> Henry Miller

It Only Recognizes Associations with Pain and Pleasure

Our critical/logical minds, as much of a deterrent as they may be, are actually very much on our sides. The one big drawback of the critical/logical mind is its limitations. When you boil it all down, all it really understands is pain and pleasure. It does its best to keep us away from anything that could cause us pain, and does its best to lead us to any person or activity that offers us pleasure. As a result, it will do its darnest to keep us away from writing. That's its job: to keep us away from anything associated with pain, and to lead us instead to pleasure. What the critical/logical mind has been taught is at the base of that constant struggle that's continually raging inside all of us. Our AW's are continually leading us to writing, while our critical/logical minds are constantly pulling us in the opposite direction.

However, what do you think would happen if you all of a sudden took a deliberate step to begin to associate pleasure with your writing? What do you think would happen? What would that do to the constant inner struggle that is at work in all of us writers? What would it do for your AW and for you as a result? The sky would then once again be the limit, just like

> *"Life is short. Live it up."*
> Nikita Khrushchev

when you were a child. But you would have the wisdom of a fully grown adult to finally take advantage of the situation. All of a sudden the personal barriers would be gone – poof! And our strongest adversary would instantly become our most staunch ally. How could this be possible though?

The Two Steps

Two steps are necessary to change any result in your life, and you've taken the first one already, which is transforming a desire into an action. Congratulations! To get this far in this book you have had to confront much. So the first step, the most challenging of the two, has already been covered.

It is the second step that needs to be looked at, examined, and put into play. That step deals with the re-associating of writing with pleasure, so that your critical/logical mind will not only start getting out of the way of your AW, but actually jumping on the bandwagon.

"We are traditionally rather proud of ourselves for having slipped creative work in there in-between the domestic chores and obligations. I'm not sure we deserve such big A-pluses for that."
Toni Morrison

To be able to succeed at the taking of the second step, it is essential that you be open and honest with the following exercise. I have found that the best way to maintain the proper attitude through the following, is just to have fun with it.

It took me years to finally get to the place where you have already gotten to in this book. And all it will take for you to break the chain of conditioning that has kept what you prize most locked away for so long is just the consistent application of that which follows.

I "Chooses"

Step 1.   Find as large of a blank, lineless piece of paper as you can. Your AW especially likes paper such as this because it is void of rules, regulations, expectations and margins. Even if all you have is an 8.5" x 11" piece of copy paper that will do fine.

Step 2. Follow the steps from earlier in this book, which suggest to you how to enter an AW connected state.

Step 3. While there, allow to come into your mind the reflection of who you were, where you were, and any significant conditions surrounding the time when you were most expressive. Once in that place, take a few deep breaths, relax and spend a few moments just communing with the reflections of yourself in the image, and how it was that you felt.

"Destiny is not a matter of chance, it is a matter of choice; it is not a thing to be waited for, it is a thing to be achieved."
William Jennings Bryan

Step 4. Then see the words *"I choose"* superimposed over the scene in your mind. Blow out any tension. Then take a moment to allow thoughts and feelings to flow into your mind in response to the words *"I choose."*

Step 5. Open your eyes, pick up your pen and write *"I choose"* any where on your piece of paper, and allow whatever response you may feel to the words to flow out next to them. Then quickly write down the words again, and allow whatever it is that you feel in response to flow out next to it. Repeat this again and again and again and again, going to a second and third page and a fourth page if you need to until you can write down *"I choose"* and nothing else comes out. This may take more than one session, but stay with it until you fully drained yourself of any responses.

Step 6. Then either extend the above exercise or repeat it by using the words *"I choose to have."*

He Gained Twelve Pounds

A number of years ago, a student of mine from Richmond, Virginia was having a challenging time getting into his AW connected state and thus the flow of his writing, as well. A lot of his dilemma stemmed from his logical, critically minded training as a CPA with an MBA.

"Angels fly because they take themselves lightly."
G. K. Chesterton

To relieve him of his struggle, I prescribed the aforementioned exercise. Then I told him to divide his responses to his "*I choose*" and "*I choose to have*" into three categories: small, medium, and large desires. I then told him to choose one item off the small list each time he completed his daily writing assignment.

Almost immediately I recognized that his writing output skyrocketed. After a few weeks exposure to this new tool, I asked him to give me an assessment of how his work with his writing was going.

"I never wrote like this before," he stated enthusiastically. *"The words are just flowing out of me. I have also found it so much easier to approach my writing each day. There is so much less of a barrier. In fact, I feel as if I have been able to move beyond whatever barriers were there to a point where I now feel completely drawn to write, no matter how it is that I am feeling physically or emotionally.*

"There is only one bad thing though," he continued.

"What's that," I asked, somewhat surprised.

"I've gained twelve pounds."

"Twelve pounds?" I questioned.

Well, what he didn't tell me was that he was using Snickers candy bars as his daily reinforcement. He also didn't inform me that the Snickers bar he chose to use as a positive reinforcement to his writing each day was one of those giant ones, the type you find at truck stops that take two hands to carry. No wonder he put on so much weight.

I couldn't convince him to stop using Snickers as his chosen form of behavior modification, but I did get him to downshift to the bite size bar instead of the gigantic one. He eventually dropped the extra weight and kept the writing style and speed, and all was well that ended well.

You Can Gain Too

Now that you have got your list, break it into the three separate categories that I mentioned previously: small, medium, and large reinforcements.

"There is no time like the pleasant."
Oliver Herford

Now, here's where the consistency comes in. Each day after you have completed one of the following writing assignments, choose something off of the small list to offer yourself as a reward. Or up until that time, any time that you read or work with this book, choose something off of the small list, as well. Use the medium list for reinforcing more extensive accomplishments, such as any one of the chapters, steps or stages laid out in this book. The last category is, of course, reserved for the completion of your rough and finished drafts or game plans, both of which will be completed by the end of this book.

It is very important that you give these reinforcements directly to yourself. The reason for this is twofold. First of all, expecting others to do for you what they may not even be able to do for themselves, or to reward you for doing something that they don't understand is unfair. Second, as you may already be beginning to understand, much of what you are and will be dealing with in this book bespeaks of learning to re-love a certain, essential aspect of yourself. So it is important that it is you that begin doing so. For no one else, no matter how hard they try, can supplement what it is that you need to do for yourself

"To the dull mind all of nature is leaden. To the illumined mind the whole world sparkles with light."
Emerson

You will not believe the "up" in your production and confidence that this technique will give you. One student that I had worked with and who had struggled something fierce to complete the draft of her first book was named Isabella.

"Isabella," I sternly reminded her, *"you have worked very, very hard to complete the writing of your work. Now it is very important that you make sure to give yourself a big reward as an acknowledgment of your accomplishment. Doing this, of course, is essential for you to begin accepting yourself as the author you are. So don't call me back until you have chosen something off of your large list and have taken the necessary steps to give whatever it is that you have chosen to yourself. So you understand?"*

"Yes," she replied.

"Okay good. Now by the time we speak again, I expect you to have taken this step. Okay?"

"Yes."

> *"We may allow ourselves a brief period of rejoicing."*
> Winston Churchill on the day WWII ended

Isabella called me back a week later and I immediately asked her if she had done as I had instructed, to which she replied that she had. I assumed that she had indeed done something special, but I was feeling nosy. I wanted to know what she had done for herself. Assuming that she had bought herself a new coat, taken herself away for a weekend or whatever, I asked, "*What was it that you did for yourself Isabella?*"

"Well, there was always this gorgeous little country cottage in England that I had always adored. So I made some calls, found the owner's name and number, and I bought it for myself over the phone."

Isabella is still writing, even today.

Negatory Stuff

> *"The most important thing is to be whatever you are without shame."*
> Rod Steiger

There's no need for any separate form of negative reinforcement if you follow the above procedures. Simply offer yourself something off one of your lists if you have accomplished your desired writing task, which in the preliminary stages, includes just reading and working with this book. Withholding what you have grown to appreciate will be enough for your critical/logical mind to begin screaming, *"Hey, we have to write today. For when we write we get that luscious cup of coffee, glass or wine or savory piece of chocolate. So let's do whatever it is that we have to do to get our person to put down on paper whatever words are necessary. You know, this writing is a good thing, because it brings us good things. So we need to keep doing it."*

What a welcome change that will be!

Chapter Eleven: Reading

"If you want to be a writer – stop talking about it and sit down and write."
Jackie Collins

It is the connection we make when we write that is so invigorating. It is this connection that teaches us about ourselves, life, and what we are all here for. It is this connection that makes us feel fulfilled, meaningful, special, loved. So powerful is this release, which comes as a result of this connection which appears after the cathartic interferences have been worn away, that the simple act of writing becomes positively addicting. What that translates to is that writing eventually becomes much harder to walk away from than it does to approach.

This form of an addiction is positive because, unlike other addictions, it feeds our lives and the desires of our soul. As a result, any author who practices AW connected writing who does not agree with the statement that writing is a narcissistic art form, is in either the worst case scenario, delusional or at least completely misinformed. For it is what we derive from that connection that keeps us coming back, refusing to

> "Readers are of two sorts; one who carefully goes through a book, and the other who as carefully lets the book go through him."
> Douglas Jerrold

forget any experience of this type, even after dozens of years have passed. It is also that which keeps us there for long periods of time, often times fighting through barrier after barrier, until the thought or feeling, seeking to manifest itself in the form of a book or screenplay, is fully released and completed.

It is this same positively addictive connection which brings us to the writings of other authors, who we vicariously live through when we are not in direct connection with our own AW's. That is why, even when during an era when so many forms of mass media and entertainment are available, we still read books. It is also the reason, even with all of the other forms of entertainment being so much easier and often cheaper to access, that we still flock to bookstores, often times spending hours there a week, and leaving at the end of a visit with our arms bulging with our purchases.

People read as they do, especially aspiring authors, because they are not fully in connection with their own AW's, as a result they have subconsciously chosen to fill that major void in their lives by living vicariously through the connections of those they choose to read. That is why we have a tendency to gravitate consistently toward one author or another. We do so because we are hearing through their works, whatever it is that our AW's are crying out to say through us. We are not connecting directly ourselves. So we are not directly hearing what is being said to us. However, in one way or another, the authors we choose to read, somehow emulate our own AW connected voice in tone, vibration, or whatever. That is what magnetizes us to their works. That attraction may feel magical and mystical but it is actually very explainable.

Thus, when we connect with our own AW's and write, we are doing for ourselves, what we have often times sought through the works of others to have done for us. It is that AW connection which draws us to our acts of writing, as well. Receiving and understanding the message or education first for yourself and then making it available to millions of others who seek to hear or experience the same message or lesson, is also how books become best sellers.

Grisham did not sit down and specifically attempt

> "He partitioned off twenty cubits at the rear of the temple with cedar boards from the floor to the ceiling to form within the temple an inner sanctuary, the Most Holy Place."
> 1 Kings 6:16

to write to the needs of tens of millions that read his first big hit *The Firm*. The same is true with King's works. In both cases, the books just flowed out of them, and in doing so, meeting their own needs and eventually the longings of the hundreds of millions whom they have touched.

The same is true for books such as the best seller *Mutant Message from Down Under* by Marlo Morgan. Like so many other books through the years, the author was unable to find a publisher for her work. With so many Fortune 500 owned houses looking for "sure bets," it is not unusual for a groundbreaking book to be overlooked.

Unable to rest until the book was released, Marlo Morgan finally self-published her work and began distributing it herself. When she did so, the sales of the book went through the roof. Then all of a sudden a suitable publisher was not difficult to find, and in no time at all this poorly written book, with the big message which mystically touched so many, was on every legitimate best-seller list in the country. The reason that all of this happened directly had to do with the AW connected message that was being shared, which transcended the author's poor style, and reached all of those hungry hearts that were clamoring for what it had to say.

> "In no other period of history were the learned so mistrusted of the divine possibilities in man as they are now."
> Gopi Krishna

Of course, your AW's message or tale that comes through you doesn't necessarily have to even end up as a book or screenplay. It can just be for personal purposes only. Thus, it doesn't have to wind up as a book that is so evolved or extraordinary that it bypasses the abilities of publishing houses to recognize it. Frankly, all books are purchased both by consumers and publishing houses, as well as screenplays by production companies, because of some unique connection either readers, editors, or producers feel to a work or to something which your AW has released through you via your writing.

So captivated was Putnam by the manuscript for *Conversations with God* by Neale Donald Walsch that they stroked him a check for over a million dollars for the rights to the book. For it was the voice and the content that came through Neale Donald Walsch's pen as he wrote his eventual best seller, that would touch off a string of best sellers, that totally captivated and grabbed this highly selective publisher's attention. This, of course, further attests to the fact that the true style and rhythm of our own AW's voice, as it is projected through us, is our strongest asset as authors.

There is also only one activity that you could participate in during the initial stages of your writing that could misdirect or prohibit that essential connection and release, and that is of your beloved reading. Notice that I said "initial." For there is no doubt that I am a committed advocate of the many benefits of reading. However, when it is done in the initial stages of writing your first work with this system it severely stunts what could and will be a very rapid and necessary transformation on your end.

The reason for this is because when you read, you are connected to voices of the AWs of other authors and not your own. When you put a temporary moratorium on your reading and begin writing, the necessary space for you to hear, feel, and experience your own AW connected voice will be created. This, of course, is essential to the effective and thus successful release of your own message. In my estimation, to get to fully know and recognize this completely essential part of yourself, takes the eventual completion of one major project. After that, you can read as many books as you would like as often as you would like, and it won't take your zest and desire away from your own writing experience. As well, from that time forward, your reading will directly benefit your writing, as what you learn from the techniques of other authors can be directly applied to your now already understood, unique and released, style and voice, which you would never have had the opportunity to experience, let alone get to know, had you not stopped reading for this relatively short period of time when you began writing.

"Educational television should be absolutely forbidden. It can only lead to unreasonable expectations and eventual disappointment when your child discovers that the letters of the alphabet do not leap out of books and dance around the room with royal-blue chickens."
Fran Lebowitz

Connection Breaker Number Eight:
To be a writer, you need to be a reader

I am confident that you can see from the above

why reading can severely disadvantage the writing of your book or screenplay using this method. As far as reading in general beyond that point, do you have to practice doing so to be a successful writer? No. For all you need will come to you and through you via your AW. In fact, you will most definitely see your desire for your beloved reading significantly drop off as you form your connection with your AW, and you no longer need to live vicariously through the communing of someone else.

So, again, no, reading is not essential to being a good writer. In fact, in the beginning stages, it can be downright counterproductive. Reading after the completion of your first work using this system forward, of course, is fine because your AW connected voice will already have been established, and you will be familiar with it. Either way though, you do not need to read to succeed as a writer. But if you enjoy doing so, by all means do so. Just wait until after you have completed your first work to fully get back into it.

> *"Do not fear death so much, but rather the inadequate life."*
> Bertolt Brecht

> *"The great thing in this works is not so much where we are, but in what direction we are moving."*
> Oliver Wendell Holmes

Cathartic Stage

In your work with "the cards", you should be beyond both the cathartic phase and through with the release of your PA's. What this means is that at least seventy percent of the index cards you are filling should be focusing on the actual storyline structure or alignment of whatever it is that you will be writing. If this is not the case, it would be best if you picked the speed by which you addressed the material on "the cards". For if your *Living Outline* is not yet beginning to fully expose itself, there is a better than excellent chance that you may pondering and thinking a bit too much, as opposed to just letting your emotions fly, which is the primary purpose with "the cards", and all writing which we will do. If this happens to be the case, give into the experience more and pick up your speed so that you may more rapidly proceed to your third stage of development before moving onto the next chapter.

Chapter Twelve: Commitment

"Obstacles are those frightful things you see when you take your eyes off your goal."
Henry Ford

Most new writers automatically jump to the conclusion that since they have not yet finished, and maybe even sold, the work that they have felt driven to write for so long, that the reason for their failure is the result of a lack of commitment on their end, which is totally and completely absurd.

The truth is that the vast majority of persons who want to write are very committed. They have experienced all sorts of success in their lives, from the acquiring of degrees, cars, homes, and other expensive possessions. To the holding down of jobs, other responsibilities, and the raising of children, not to mention all of the stick-to-it-ness they have had with their writing, no matter how little financial or personal success it may have offered them.

The tens of thousands of aspiring writers that I have had the distinct pleasure to be in the company of are very committed people. Most just have not properly

Tom Bird - ~~Write~~ Right From God

committed themselves and their fine energies to that which they want to do with their writing. That is the reason they have not succeeded.

So, from my perspective, you don't have to commit more to gain the success you seek with your writing. You simply have to commit more effectively to garner the results which you aspire to.

"He who hesitates is a damned fool."
Mae West

The Contract

There is one common denominator between each and every success, no matter how small or large, that you have experienced in your life. That common denominator is the fact that, in one way or another, you have entered into some form of agreement with yourself, and most probably an outside source or two that directly led to the successful completion of whatever the task happened to be. Now, if that has worked so successfully and consistently with everything else that you have succeeded with in your life, why have you not rooted the same technique into your work with your beloved writing? I have found that a contract or an agreement is almost always the difference between success and failure for an aspiring author.

Before I get into the basics of your contract, allow me to first say that logistically this will be the simplest step that you will be asked to take. You can write it in longhand, type it out, whatever, as long as it is committed to paper, copied, and distributed in the manner suggested. All of this, including the mailing of it, will cost you less than five dollars and take you less than an hour, travel time included, to complete. Why then does it often take a less aspiring writer than yourself weeks, if not months, to often complete?

"Writing is turning one's worst moments into money."
J.P.Donleavy

The reason that it often takes so long for a writer to complete this necessary step is because it is far, and away, the most emotionally challenging of all tasks in this book. For there is a distinct difference between talking about writing than actually doing it.

Most of you have been talking about what you were going to do with your writing for years, if not decades, and where has it gotten you? Nowhere, until you came to your senses and sought the age old advice and wise counsel housed in this book. However, the reason that you have now taken so seriously your commitment to follow through with your claims about writing is because there is a part of you that knows that whatever guides , or whatever you like to guide, your life will fully get behind your efforts once they are finally committed to paper. Here comes that old fear of success again. For this side has listened to all of your empty, verbal claims in the past, and amazingly still has faith in you after hundreds if not thousands of what could be viewed as let downs. This side has begun to associate action with commitment, which means words, promises committed to paper. It has also grown tired and learned to ignore the verbal rantings, which have done nothing up to this point but to take up valuable time and energy. The side of yourself to which I refer is your AW.

> "You gain strength, courage and confidence by every experience in which you really stop to look fear in the face. You are able to say to yourself, 'I've lived through this horror. I can take the next thing that comes along.' You must do the thing you think you cannot do."
> Eleanor Roosevelt

You may recall my tale from earlier in the book about the advice I received from the learned sports writer named Dick Young in which he offered me the sage wisdom of *"just write."* Having run out of more convenient and less challenging alternatives, I finally decided to accept Dick's advice a few weeks later. Upon doing so, I laid out a production pace for myself to write daily for six months. Every day the number of words that I wrote would grow until I was writing 7,000 words a day. In actuality, I was finally releasing my fate to my AW. I had finally come to the simple, but exact, understanding that *"writers are people who write."* The connection that I had not made, up to that point, was that it was from that simple, committed activity from which I would eventually draw my strength, wisdom, guidance, voice and, most of all, the passion that spoke through me as I transcended the confines of my own critical/logical mind.

Of course, if you recall the aforementioned, you also recall the results that I was met with next. By the end of my six month agreement with myself, I completed my first book, while working a job in which I put in over 90 hours a week. I also landed the finest literary representative in the country who sold my book to the third largest publisher in the world. The sale enabled me to resign from my job with over three years salary in the bank.

Up until that point, I was like every other aspiring author. I had taken the classes, read all of the books, and talked incessantly about writing all of the time, but I hadn't put it all on the line, turned it over to and committed to the author of that longtime desire in me – my AW. Once I did, I finally got out of my own way by handing the responsibility of my own success to that which drove me, but which had frightened me because I could not see it with my own eyes and touch it with my own hands, and could only feel with my heart. It was then, and only after that move, that what I aspired to be, and what I felt that I was inside already, could come to life.

I follow the same procedures any time that I write a book even today. I break the composition and completion of the blessed task into the stages that I have shared and will continue to share with you, and then commit to them in writing. The rest takes care of itself immediately afterwards.

I do the same with my students, as well. In fact, I will not work with a student who refuses to commit to their own success in writing. The reason for that is by not committing to and guiding and releasing their own success in writing, they are admitting to an unreadiness and an unwillingness, to live their dreams. It's obviously just not their time yet. Maybe they haven't yet suffered enough through exposure to those methods which do not work. It is a common belief in many circles that a person doesn't make the necessary changes in his or her life until the pain has gotten so great that they finally have to make the necessary alterations, overcome their fears, and just do so. I am a very firm believer in this, as well.

When I first began individually mentoring students on the writing of their books and screenplays, I did so purely on a scholarship basis. However, I had to stop doing so after a few months. The reason that I had to quit doing so was because those students with whom I was working, drained me emotionally. They were all excuses and no writing. It was then that I

"You can't win any game unless you are ready to win."
Connie Mack

"No wind favors him who has no destined port."
Michel De Montaigne

realized that the mistake that I had made with them was that I had not made them commit to their intentions in writing. My pain and suffering which came as the result of their lack of production came to an abrupt halt after that, when I let go of all of them and refused to take on any students who would not only commit to their work in writing but commit to working with me with their monies, as well. The difference between the two populations was astounding. The miracle that I knew was present in all of us immediately began to spring forth in the second group while those of the initial group continued to die on the vine.

I openly admit in my seminars that my most daunting task is to get those in attendance to actually commit to their own success through the entering into an agreement with themselves. As part of the class, I invite each of the attendees to cement their commitments by sending me a copy of their agreement, sort of a formal right of passage. I realize that those who send me a contract stand a very high chance of completing their books. I also realize that those who are not ready to enter into a contract, are not, and may not ever be ready emotionally, to take that step. Many of the latter group end up retaking my class at some point down the road, or just wind up living vicariously through the lives, dreams, and words of others. That is how important this step is for you. Do it and you will in all likelihood succeed. Avoid it and you probably won't. From all of my experience and study that is what I have learned.

Before the Contract

"Blessed is the man who has found his work."
Elbert Hubbard

Before moving forward with the specific elements of the contract you now know is essential to your success, it is important to generate as much true enthusiasm as possible to take into it. It is best that this enthusiasm is based on understanding, confidence, vision, trust, and faith. Otherwise, it will wear off as quickly as the pre-game hype all football players have until they suffer their first on field hit. To generate that which is necessary and which will allow you to accept, as opposed to attempt to stop, the reckless abandon and enthusiasm of your AW, it is important that you will have worked with your cards all the way up through the third phase where the *Living Outline* has been released and tacked up on your bulletin board. The successful completion of the aforementioned will significantly lessen your struggle. For your critical/logical mind needs to see to believe, before it can give into the possibility of anything of significance actually appearing out of you. So not only will your critical/logical mind finally begin to back off, enabling you to rid yourself of that unnecessary weight, but you will simply believe in the process so much more after the actual book you have felt drawn to write has magically appeared in outline form before your very eyes. It will just make taking this next step so much easier and thus so much more possible. So if you haven't already done so, complete the final phase of your work with "the cards" before moving onto the next section.

Your Written Commitment to Living Your Dream – Signed and Dated

As you will see through the examples of contracts that I have included at the end of this chapter, each one of the agreements is signed and dated. Your agreement needs to be signed and dated, as well.

As is true with any of the individual components of your contract, each element which makes it up should convey as much passion as possible. For it is this passion that your critical/logical mind will especially feed off of as it gets behind you via your contract. The more excited it is, the more momentum it will generate for you out of the starting blocks.

It is also important to be as personally expressive as possible when writing this contract. Remember, this is an agreement that you are writing, but one of a deeply personal nature, so allow it to bespeak of that. Don't try to be an attorney or anyone else but your most expressive self when writing this agreement. Just be you, which is what this drill and this entire

"Losers visualize the penalties of failure. Winners visualize the rewards of success."
Dr. Rob Gilbert

"What the world needs is more geniuses with humility. There are so few of us left."
Oscar Levant

book is about anyway.

General Statement of Purpose

Every agreement, no matter how small or large, has to have a general statement of purpose, which basically answers the question, *"what is it that you are promising to do?"*

In this case, if you are going to write a book or screenplay, state that. If you are going to write something different or do something other than that, state that instead. How long should you give yourself to complete it, is in question. Let's go over that.

There is productive pressure and counterproductive pressure. Productive pressure gets you off your duff and motivates you through the successful completion of a task. Counterproductive pressure proves too heavy. In this case it would chart too short of a deadline, which would force you to give up, possibly even before you even get started. In your situation, there is more than a good chance that you haven't had any positive pressure in regard to whatever it is you want to complete as the result of this contract, which is one of the primary reasons for this contract.

Before we get into specific time frames, let me share a few other points with you. First of all, in choosing a time frame to complete your work, I would strongly recommend that you *not* take into consideration what you have heard from other sources outside of this program. The reason for that is that their propositions and estimations, and thus results have been partially or wholly based on the erroneous thought patterns and beliefs that eventually led you to the acquisition of this book in the first place. So I would not consider them as viable sources of consideration when calculating the time frame you will utilize as your deadline for completion.

Second, I strongly suggest that you more heavily weight that which is possible in a best case scenario and minimize your concerns over the worst case alternative when calculating your deadline. In other words, I suggest you stay away from the thinking of what is

> *"Only the curious will learn and only the resolute overcome the obstacles of learning. The quest quotient has always excited me more than the intelligence quotient."*
> Eugene S. Wilson

possible in your current situation, and instead more strongly take into consideration what would be possible after some alternations in your typical routine take place. The reason for my suggestion in this regard is because, as stated previously, the minute that you enter into this agreement big things and big changes will begin to happen for you. As your AW takes over and gets behind the wheel amazing results will happened; all of a sudden, out of nowhere, something will clear in your routine, and you'll find the two hours you need to write daily. Because you now have a pleasurable reason to get up, maybe rising will no longer be a burden; or any other number of things that you may thought to be difficult or incurable will be taken care of, without you even lifting a finger.

Third, speed, as we will more thoroughly get into in a later chapter, is very important to consider if writing a book or screenplay is what you desire to do. What it all boils down to is this: the faster that you write your book or screenplay, the less time you have to "think," which is, of course, a derivative of the critical/logical mind. This all translates to: keeping any potential critical/logical mind distractions to a minimum by writing as fast as you can so that you don't have any time to think.

What speed does that translate to? On a weekly basis, writing two hours a day, six days a week, at 1200 words an hour – which is the lowest speed at which your AW will express itself, translates to about 15,000 words a week. The average length of an adult book-length manuscript is 80,000 words, which would mean that it would take you approximately five and a half weeks to arrive at that total.

In coming up with a more exact figure for this, simply compare the length of books that have already been written in the same area. What is the average length? How do you come up with an understanding of that in terms of a number of words?

To do so, pick out one or two of these books and turn to what appears to be an average page or two. Count the number of words on these few pages and them simply multiply the average number that you arrive at by the number of pages in the book. Do this

"In life, as in football, you won't go far unless you know where the goalposts are."
Arnold Glasow

for more than one work, and then come up with an average for the books that you used, and you have the average number of words that you should be shooting for.

When you review the sample contract at the conclusion of this chapter, you will see that they vary widely between the contracts that my students typically write in designing a working arrangement for the mentoring of themselves, and those who instead chose to employ me in that role. The reason for that is because under my tutelage, I estimate the speed that my students will be able to routinely write to be at about 1500 words an hour, which is the average rate at which the AW releases. While being taken under my wing, as well, I can also delete some of the steps my students would normally be required to take on their own. So there is absolutely no way that you should be ashamed if, while using the figures below, you come up with a span of six months to complete your first book. That is still darn fast. In fact, just about any famous author would be proud of that.

Fourth, concerning the final facts and figures in regard to your contractual time frame, there are several considerations to take into account.

The actual first step of your contract should be based upon the actual *Living Outline* being completed, which should already be completed by now. So no time needs to be allotted there.

The time frame for the successful completion of the second step should be comprised of how long it will take you to complete the releasing of the rough draft or rough arrangements for whatever it is which you want to do. By now, you should have come up with an appropriate expected length for your work, based upon the information that was discussed earlier in this chapter. If you have not done that yet, go ahead and do so now. Once you have that total, divide that figure by 1,200 words, which will tell you approximately how many hours it will take you to complete it. Then divide the total number of hours that you are estimating that it will take you to complete your work by the number of hours you are allotting to write each week, which will give you an approximate for the number of weeks

> "The high prize of life, the crowning fortune of a man, is to be born with a bias to some pursuit which finds him in employment and happiness."
> Emerson

Tom Bird - ~~Write~~ Right From God

that you will take to do the job.

Steps Three and Four normally take two and three weeks respectively. So then plug in those two numbers.

The last figure that we are responsible for coming up with is the one for how long it will take you to complete chapters seven through thirteen. I suggest reserving two weeks until you have completed Part Two and you are then ready to enter into Part Three in which your project will actually be released, perfected, and completed.

With all of the above completed, you are now ready to list the time frames for each categorical consideration for defining the time frame for the completion of your project. Add up all of them, and then multiply the total time you come up with by thirty percent, and add this figure onto your previous sum to come up with your final time frame. The reason that I suggest adding on an extra thirty percent is to insure that you make whatever deadline it is that you set. Doing so will produce more for your confidence than anything else. Missing your deadline would, of course, give your critical/logical mind the open shot it has been looking for to strike home with its unfair comments and taunts.

Again, there is a fine line between positive pressure and its negative counterpart. Completing your work within the time frame you came up with plus an additional thirty percent is positive pressure, that compassionately makes room for further necessary personal transitions and real to life situations that may just happen to pop up that may need to be dealt with. You have come far to get to where you are by this point. You are far from a failure, and you are surely committed and driven, and rewarding your efforts with considerations of this sort need to be consistently addressed from this point forward.

Congratulations for coming this far. Plus, if you do not need to use your thirty percent overflow to meet your deadline, you can see that as even more of a major, personal victory. In that case, you can present yourself with an even larger reward.

"To love what you do and feel that it matters – how could anything be more fun?"
Katherine Graham

"When a fantasy turns you on, you're obligated to God and nature to start doing it – right away."
Stewart Brand

The Wager

An agreement of any sort is a wager with yourself. and others, to complete a task for the acquisition of something you truly want or need. In that regard, you are awarded with positive reinforcements upon the successful completion of your agreement. The opposite is true, of course, with the negative reinforcements that are set in place. It is the correct balance between these two forces, the positive and the negative, both of which are catalysts for our actions, that give us our best opportunity to reach our goal.

After you complete your agreement, it would be best for you to make seven copies of it. Keep the first copy for yourself and insure that this document is in open view each and every time you practice in the completion of your chosen task. Take it with you when you travel and make sure it is openly displayed wherever your work space may be, whether that is at home, at your office, or wherever. There will be times when you will forget and would best be reminded why it is that you are doing what you are, and it's the job of your contract to do just that.

> *"Never give in. Never. Never. Never."*
> Sir Winston Churchill

Send the second copy to me. Why? This is a formal right of passage that you would be best to experience by offering it to me, your mentor, so that you may build an even greater acceptance of yourself. The extra boost in awareness, confidence, and self esteem through doing so will create tremendous momentum for you.

When I receive the contract, I will drop you a line in response, wishing you luck and acknowledging your agreement. Please, please, please, let me know, as well when you have completed your work. Since I actually get to know so few of you on a personal basis, I also miss the chance to celebrate along with you when your projects are completed if you don't send me a copy of your agreement.

If you don't already have my mailing address, it is: P.O. Box 4306., Sedona, AZ 86336. You can also fax me at 928/203-0264 or e-mail me through my website at www.ambassu.com. Feel free to use any of the above means to contact me both with your contract and to inform me when you have completed you book or screenplay.

> "The thing always happens that you really believe in; and the belief in a thing makes it happen."
> Frank Lloyd Wright

There have been many influences that have carried you to this point, and not all of them have created pleasant, reassuring memories. However, the truth is that you are still substantially motivated by the pressure of avoiding failure. There are persons who tangibly represent this fact in your life right now. There always have been. You know the one I am talking about. The aunt, uncle, friend, colleague, sibling, or even parent who continually told you, against the calling of your own heart, that you couldn't do what it is that you are just about to do. In an odd and uncomfortable way, each of these persons have contributed to your success. The are now just about to make their largest and most significant contribution, though, when you send three of these persons a copy of your agreement to complete your dream project.

I realize that this may sound ludicrous to you. However, there will days when you will not be at your best, and during which time you will not feel like writing. It is during these stretches, when your consistent approach to your writing will be so paramount that the fear of potentially having to face them with bad news will be the only motivator that will be able to get you back on track. Then is the time to allow them to be the assets that they always wanted to be but which they just didn't know how to go about doing so.

> "I only have "yes" men around me. Who needs "no" men?
> Mae West

The last two copies of your agreement are to be sent to two persons who love you unconditionally. The reason for sending it to them is for consistent, moral support, no matter what it is that you are experiencing.

With each and every agreement that you send out, it is paramount that you make a promise to each person, and state it in the contract, that you send it to. Promise to give them something or to give up something that you would hate to lose if you do not complete your ultimate task, or any of the steps along the way. I know that this may sound difficult to do. However, even more difficult is the reversing of your past behavior patterns without re-approaching these conditioned habits without the right ammunition.

This contract will allow you to do all that you want to do with your writing. Utilize it in exactly the format that I have discussed and you will meet with a success beyond your wildest expectations.

Before Moving On

The next chapter begins a series of chapters that will directly prepare you for your actual writing, which will begin in Part Three. Before moving on, it is essential to make sure that you have fully completed and posted your *Living Outline* through your work with "the cards", and that you have completed and sent out all the necessary copies of your contracts. If you have not already completed these tasks, do so before going to the chapter.

What Does This All Have to do With Connection Breaker Number Nine: *You need to be committed to do any good with your writing?*

There are obviously many misnomers associated with writing. One of the most ridiculous, though, is the one which states that you have to be disciplined to be a successful writer. No matter how you choose to define the former, you only need to be disciplined if you are either doing something that you don't like to do, or if you are attempting to do something which you are frightened to do.

By the very fact that you have arrived this far into this book, I assume, that for one reason or another, writing even if that translates to just recently, at one time or another has somehow benefited you. So the first case for discipline is already satisfied.

In regard to being frightened to write, that is what we have been attacking with this chapter. The truth is that you will always be frightened to write, no matter how many books or screenplays you write and sell, unless time is taken to re-associate writing with

"The only man who is really free is the one who can turn down an invitation to dinner without giving an excuse."
Jules Renard

"When you cease to take a contribution you begin to die."
Eleanor Roosevelt

pleasure. Then and only then will you be able to project what you enjoy so much to the fullest. Once that step is taken, not only will you find it so much easier to do more often what you enjoy so much, but you will do it much better, and thus much more successfully as a result.

Sample Contracts

INTENSIVE WRITER PROGRAM AGREEMENT #1

Tom Bird and Author──────────── whose address is

hereby agree to as follows:

Intensive Writing Program

A. Services To Be Rendered – Consultation and Review:

1. Mr. Bird shall provide an average of 4 consultations per week, specifically designed to lead and guide the author to the successful completion and revision of his or her books.

2. Mr. Bird shall upon completion, review the draft of the Author's two manuscripts (two maximum), for the specific purpose of refining them for publication. Each manuscript will be reviewed and commented upon no more than twice each.

3. Once the author's manuscript(s) is/are in a fully completed and finished form, Mr. Bird shall assist the author in the composition of his or her query letter package; all components of his or her submission package to be submitted to prospective literary agents; provide a listing of literary agents and consult with the author on the choice of prospective literary agents; consult with the author on any suggestions or rewrite marketing strategies suggested by prospective literary agents and serve as a marketing liaison between the author and the author's publisher, aggressively pursuing the goal of obtaining an appropriate publisher for the author's work.

B. Compensation

Mr. Bird shall be paid a non-refundable fee of ($_____)

If Mr. Bird chooses to allow payments, 25% of the above fee shall be due immediately with the remaining payments divided over no more than six months, with each payment coming due on the _____ of each month. If any of the aforementioned payments are received more than 10 days after the due date, a 10% late fee will be paid by the author.

If the author cancels out of this agreement before it's completion Mr. Bird will immediately be due his entire fee.

C. Other

If the author chooses to continue to consult with Mr. Bird after the conclusion of the consultation period set forth above, such further participation and consultation, both as to how and for how long, will be negotiated separately.

D. Default

All costs, attorneys' fees, and other expenses of enforcing this agreement shall be paid to the prevailing party by the losers, including collection fees and costs.

Acknowledged and agreed to by: _____

Author_____   Thomas J. Bird_____

Date   Date

INTENSIVE WRITER PROGRAM AGREEMENT #2

Tom Bird and Author, ———————————— whose address is: ——————————————————————————————

hereby agree to as follows:

Intensive Writing Program

A. Services To Be Rendered – Consultation and Review:

1. Mr. Bird shall provide an average of 4 consultations per week, specifically designed to lead and guide the author to the successful completion and revision of his or her books.

2. Mr. Bird shall upon completion, review the draft of the Author's two manuscripts (two maximum), for the specific purpose of refining them for publication. Each manuscript will be reviewed and commented upon no more than twice each.

3. Once the author's manuscript(s) is/are in a fully completed and finished form, Mr. Bird shall assist the author in the composition of his or her query letter package; all components of his or her submission package to be submitted to prospective literary agents; provide a listing of literary agents and consult with the author on the choice of prospective literary agents; consult with the author on any suggestions or rewrite marketing strategies suggested by prospective literary agents and serve as a marketing liaison between the author and the author's publisher, aggressively pursuing the goal of obtaining an appropriate publisher for the author's work.

B. Compensation

In addition to the commission set forth below Mr. Bird shall be paid a nonrefundable fee of ($_____), which comprises a reduction from $_____, which would comprise Mr. Bird's regular fee for such a service.

If Mr. Bird chooses to allow payments, 25% of the above fee shall be due immediately with the remaining payments divided over no more than six months, with each payment coming due on the _____ of each month. If any of the aforementioned payments are received more than 10 days after the due date, a 10% late fee will be paid by the author.

In consideration of lowering of Mr. Bird's regular fee, Mr. Bird shall be entitled to a commission on the amounts received by author as to said publication which shall be as follows:

(a) First Book: A commission of Fifteen Percent (15%) upon the gross proceeds received by the author on the first book, screenplay, or any other major work produced as a result of the consultation provided above.

(b) Second Book: A Ten Percent (10%) commission upon the gross proceeds received by the author of his or her second book, screenplay, or any other major work.

The only other fees for which the author will be responsible for are those which cover out-of-pocket expenses in regards to presentation of the author's work to literary agents and/or publishers. Any copy editing and/or out of pocket expenses which exceed Twenty ($20.00) dollars shall require the prior approval of the author.

If the author changes his or her mind and chooses not to submit his or her work for publication or fails to consistently follow the guidance of Mr. Bird and thus does not complete his or her works, Mr. Bird will immediately be due the total amount of his regular fee.

C. Other

If the author chooses to continue to consult with Mr. Bird after the conclusion of the consultation period set forth above, such further participation and consultation, both as to how and for how long, will be negotiated separately.

D. Default

All costs, attorneys' fees, and other expenses of enforcing this agreement shall be paid to the prevailing party by the losers, including collection fees and costs.

Acknowledged and agreed to by:

_____   _____
Author   Thomas J. Bird

_____   _____
Date   Date

INDIVIDUAL CONTRACT

On this seventh (7th) day of October in the year 2001, I (Author), do enter into this contract willingly and with full knowledge of what is expected of me by me. I write this contract in order to commit myself to writing a book, a book that is presently inside of me now. I will complete this book by Thanksgiving of the year 2001. I do understand the necessity of this contract binding me to a commitment of writing.

I will reserve two hours daily, six days a week to write.

I will remove all distractions. I will set boundaries of those near and dear to me to respect those boundaries so that I may have uninterrupted time.

I will do relaxing exercises before writing, while writing, and after writing.

I will allow my thoughts and feelings to flow freely on blank index cards.

I will post my results on a bulletin board on the wall above my desk.

I will make a list of all that I would like to have and do.

I will break then into daily, weekly actions.

On a daily basis I will reward myself with a cigarette and O'Doules (even if it is 10 o'clock in the morning) on the patio.

When I have made a completion of one step I will treat myself and my children, to a full course lobster meal at a restaurant.

When I have finished my final copy and have sent it off to the Literary Agent I will travel to Sedona and spend the day, complete with a picnic lunch of my favorite foods on the back site of Oak Creek Canyon, I will take pictures and rejoice in my favorite place. I will take my son and daughter if possible.

I gladly and willingly and most excitedly do sign this contract.

_____   _____
Author   Date

Chapter Thirteen:
The Wider the Space, the More Passionate the Expression, the Better the Writing

"The artist is nothing without the gift, but the gift is nothing without work."
Emile Zola

    Passion of the heart that forms the bridge between that which our AWs represent and us, and then between us and our readers. It is this same exact component that entices the hearts and minds of persons everywhere, from literary agents to editors, publishers, movie production executives and, of course, readers and viewers in general. Thus, if you want to author, what you get paid for is the passion that is released through you when you write.

    Passion is also not something that you can edit into a project. Either it's there or it's not. So absolutely important is this one ingredient to the quality of your work, that in welcoming the carrier of the necessary passion into your writing, it would make sense to insure that as comfortable of a space be provided for this relay as possible. For the more comfortable he or she is, the more deeply and expressively our carriers will perform, allowing your project to have the communicative life and vibrancy which it seeks.

What the AW Craves

Your carrier, your AW, is a freedom seeker. Being unconditional in nature, it seeks the wide open spaces. That is why both the lineless side of "the cards" and the large lineless pieces of paper you have been using have worked so well up to this point.

Over the last two decades, I have seen these large, lineless pieces of paper work miracles. On more than several occasions, I have had aspiring authors enter my classes or seminars suffering from what they thought to be incurable writer's block. For months, sometimes years, these persons had not been able to write anything of worth. Needless to say, by the time they finally got around to taking one of my courses, they were at best unnerved or distraught. In each case, I offered them hope through a writing exercise.

Then just before our appointed time to begin the writing exercise, I would hand out to each student a blank, lineless, 22" x 28" piece of poster board. Simply because of the enormity of this piece of blank paper, there was no one in class who wasn't feeling uneasy or nervous, especially those suffering from the dreaded "creative constipation." Unbeknownst to them, though, it is their critical/logical minds that are creating their reaction. For the lack of lines, tangible barriers, rules and regulations, and margins is scaring their critical/logical minds to death.

However, I have yet, in all the thousands of classes that I have taught over the last two decades, to see when the *Three R's of Writing* are used in conjunction with the poster boards where writer's block is not cured instantly. I have seen many a literary miracle take place, including long-awaited outlines for books or screenplays, or entire books or screenplays, released immediately.

"God, give us the grace to accept with serenity the things that cannot be changed, courage to change the things which should be changed, and the wisdom to distinguish the one from the other."
Reinhold Niebuhr, 1943

"Our greatest happiness does not depend on the condition of life in which chance has placed us, but is always the result of a good conscience, good health, occupation, and freedom in all just pursuits."
Thomas Jefferson

The reason for these astounding results is very logical. Your AW, the holder of what it is that has been waiting and yearning to be released through you for years, craves unconditional space and freedom, and thus it loves the lineless poster boards.

William Faulkner was aware of this fact, which is why he wrote his books on the walls of his home. Walt Disney was familiar with this technique, too, which is why he did all of his sketching and planning on large pieces of poster board sized paper.

Where did their genius come from, you may have wondered? It did not come from their own minds, but instead from the decisions they made to venture outside the realms of their selves to connect, in the most conducive way possible, with that which had been calling to them from beyond their human limitations.

I came upon the brilliance of this dynamic technique simply through listening to my own AW, which led me to the concept. Once I began using "the boards", I could not believe the ease, depth, speed, direction, and passion by which my words and works flowed out of me.

"My parents have been visiting me for a few days. I just dropped them off at the airport. They leave tomorrow."
Margaret Smith

Why This Works

Your AW longs for an intimate connection with you. It calls for its feelings, its depth, and its passion to be expressed through you and reflected back to it through you, so that it may best gauge the significance and effectiveness of its release. The only way that this can be accomplished is through direct connection with the very fiber and essence of the expression itself.

Sculptors do this by becoming one with their work. They see an image calling to be released from a stone or piece of granite, which they seek to free with their hammers and chisels. In the process, they breathe, swallow, and become covered in the dust of their passions.

Painters follow the same process. At the conclusion of any productive painting session, they too, are covered in the residue of their expressions.

By employing the methods in this book, and espe-

"Here is the test to find whether your mission on earth is finished: if you're alive, it isn't."
Richard Bach

cially in this chapter, you will be offered the same freeing and necessary opportunity, as well. However, instead of using a chisel, or a hammer, or a paint brush, or pastels to release the passion that seeks to be released through you, you will use a pen to write on "the boards".

In choosing the correct writing utensil, it is important to keep in mind that the more ink that gets to the tip of your pen the better. For the more ink which is available, the faster your result will be, and the faster you are able to relay whatever it is that is coming through you, the easier it will be for you to keep up with your AW's enlightened speed of expression.

> "His is his own best friend, and takes delight in privacy; whereas the man of no virtue or ability is his own worst enemy and is afraid of solitude."
> Aristotle

But I Can't Read my Writing When I Write in Longhand

Initially, one of the most common concerns that I receive from my students about using "the boards" is that they won't be able to read their own handwriting.

Right now, for whatever reasons, you may find yourself partially or fully compromised at several essential junctures in your life. As a result, you may have become disconnected with the intentions of your AW.

When we are confused, lost or frightened, which is a direct result of compromise, we have a tendency to roll ourselves up in a tight, little ball and to hide away. This sort of disposition is reflected in the presentation of ourselves through our handwriting, as well. It curls itself real tight, in an effort to become invisible, and thus it becomes nearly impossible to read. Or your true self disguises itself through your writing not becoming too small to be read, but illegible instead.

Our handwriting and how we approach it, says much about us. In fact, one way to gauge the comfort and confidence by which your AW is being released comes through your use of margins. How close you begin your writing to your left margin is a direct reflection of how well you have dealt with past emotional issues that could possibly hold you back. How far you write over to the right margin is a direct reflec-

> "The people who get on in this work are the people who get up and look for the circumstances they want, and, if they can't find them, make them."
> George Bernard Shaw

tion of how confidently and comfortably you are projecting yourself toward your future as a result.

Thank God that limiting tendencies that you may exude in your use of the margins can be reversed simply by working with your own handwriting, insuring to start as close to the left hand margin as possible while projecting yourself as far to the right hand margin as you can. These two simple adjustments to your handwriting will do wonders for the freedom that your AW expresses itself.

But I Type so Much Faster and Write so Much Better at the Keyboard

"If someone says 'can't' that shows you what to do."
John Cage

The computer age has offered us much, including keyboard dependency.

It is not that we were born with the innate ability to type faster than we can write in longhand. We have simply, through our over exposure to the keyboard, often learned to type faster than we can write in longhand.

I would be a full proponent of the typing of all of your writing if it actually worked to your benefit, but it doesn't. In fact, attempting to release your manuscripts through a keyboard is one of the most glaring reasons for the failure of the aspiring writer.

The reason for that fact is that by composing your work at the keyboard, you are innocently violating much of what your AW needs to do its job. When composing at the keyboard, the direct connection between the AW and its words is severed. No longer is its direct, unconditional message reflected back to it, which it craves, for the computer or typewriter that you are using gets in the way.

The dependence on your computer screen also robs your AW of the ability it seeks to view large expansions of its expressions at a single glance. As a result, there is no way for your AW to gauge the significance of what it is saying in comparison to what it has said and what it is going to say. In doing so, your computer robs your AW of the necessary perspective for which it longs. Without that, it has a tendency to lose it place, forget what it has said, and to repeat the same themes over and over again, and thus becoming redundant.

Of course, you may like writing at the keyboard much more than writing in longhand. This is only natural because of the fact that you spend so much more time composing in that manner. However, this does not make using the keyboard superior to the results that can be achieved through writing in longhand on "the boards". If you would simply write in longhand on "the boards" as much as you have on the keyboard, you will find that the former will become just as, if not more, comfortable than its automated counterpart.

> "Lots of folks confuse bad management with destiny."
> Kim Hubbard

Lineless Alternatives

There are three basic facts that are most important to keep in mind when choosing a lineless writing surface for your writing: 1) the larger the better; 2) it must be sturdy to enable it to survive normal wear and tear and the reversionary stage; and 3) travel ability.

Here are the alternatives which I can suggest.

- *Flip Charts. This alternative is relatively inexpensive, costing approximately the same per sheet as the poster boards. They are also light weight and travel easy. However, their one drawback is their durability, since they rip and tear easily.*

- *Drawing Pads. These are not usually as big as the flip charts or the poster boards. However, they are durable, travel easy and run about the same price.*

- *Poster Boards. These are my recommendations because they are inexpensive if you buy them in a ten pack from a national, office supply chain and durable. They are the least convenient for travel though, which is their one drawback.*

> "Faith is the bird that feels the light and sings when the dawn is still dark"
> Rabindranath Togore

Connection Breaker Number Ten:
One should write on lined pads of paper or on a typewriter or via a computer word processing program.

This chapter directly confronts the misunderstanding of CB# 10: One should write on lined pads of paper, or on a typewriter, or via a computer word processing program. For as I have made clear, the AW frees itself most unconditionally on large, lineless sheets of paper. The bigger the better. The bigger, the more passion. Passion is the essential communicative link between you and your AW, and your readers as well, if you choose to share your work.

> *"If you have anything really valuable to contribute to the world it will come through the expression of your own personality, that single spark of divinity that sets you off and makes you different from every other living creature."*
> Bruce Barton

Your Assignment

It's now time for you to go out and purchase your chosen writing surface. On your shopping list, also make sure to include the purchase of whatever pen you choose to use, and possibly a back-up, as well.

In regard to the quantity of writing surfaces to purchase, buy enough to complete the writing of your entire screenplay or book. What that translates to is at least 120 sheets of either the flip charts or poster boards, or nearly twice as many if you are buying a drawing pad.

Do not move onto the next chapter until you have completed this absolutely essential task.

Chapter Fourteen:
Essential Suggestions to Live By

"It is only the farmer who faithfully plants seeds in the Spring, that reaps a harvest in the Autumn."
B.C. Forbes

By now, you should have purchased both plenty of sheets of your chosen writing surface and your pens. If you have not done this yet, do so before reading any further into this chapter.

As you were picking out and buying your writing surface and pens, you may have felt exhilarated or nervous. The latter comes from your critical/logical mind's reaction to the task it feels lies before it with the lineless paper. However, what it does not know yet or understand, is that we will not be calling upon it to do anything. Any exhilaration that you may have felt, of course, came from your AW, which just can't wait to get started.

However, when you do get started your critical/logical mind may over react and attempt to do whatever it can do to keep you from entering the dangerous space that it believes exists when you write. So initially it may do its best to drag you away from your writing whenever possible.

Its usual modus operandi is to distract you from your writing by posing many a concern. Not at least acknowledging what it has to say will only make matters worse for you, which is why so many who have adhered to CB #11, which states *"Always stay within the lines of what it is that you are writing about"* and have experienced their writing coming to an abrupt halt via the dreaded writer's block.

All that is needed is a space reserved for the critical/logical mind to initially voice its concerns so that they don't become a distraction and eventually a roadblock to what the AW has to say.

This potential dilemma is easily cured by creating a loosely drawn, one inch, right hand column on the side of each one of your writing surfaces. Whenever a thought pops up that is unrelated to your writing, such as *"don't forget to pick up bananas at the market,"* simply toss it over into the space provided in the narrow column and keep going. This pattern will allow the critical/logical mind to express itself without interrupting the flow of your AW.

"Gratitude is not only the greatest of virtues, but the parent of all the others."
Cicero

I Am Thankfuls

Step 1. Take the necessary steps to place yourself in your AW connected state, insuring that some of your newly purchased writing surfaces are within arms length as well as your new writing utensils.

Step 2. After achieving your necessary AW connected state, write on your chosen writing surface the words *"I am thankful"* and then allow yourself to freely associate a response. Then write the words *"I am thankful"* again and formulate a second response. Continue to do this as fast as possible until you have completely filled up one of your writing surfaces.

No Edit, No Read, Just Write

> "What if everything is an illusion and nothing exists? In that case, I definitely overpaid for my carpet."
> Woody Allen

It is not that your critical/logical mind is without a true and definite purpose. However, there is a specific time and place for its attributes to be properly employed, but during any writing or composing of your initial AW based expressions is not the place. The reason for this is that the critical/logical mind's discriminating interaction will choke off your connection with your AW.

When one follows the inappropriate advice of CB #12, which states *"To produce good writing one has to carefully search for mistakes as he or she goes,"* your essential connection with your AW, and its voice, is stifled.

Thus, it is important to avoid, at all costs, editing or looking for mistakes when you are writing. There will be plenty of time for that later. But it is to be avoided until your arrive at that place further down the road. Simply allow your AW to express freely and openly in the space you have provided for it to do so. If the critical/logical mind has anything to say, allow it to be said in the narrow, right hand column you have created for it to do so.

I Wish

Step 1. Slip into your AW connected state, making sure that your chosen writing surface and new pens are nearby.

Step 2. Follow the same instructions for the last writing exercise. However, instead of directing your expression with the words "*I am thankful,*" lead instead with the words "*I wish.*" Fill at least one sheet of your chosen writing surface, or more if you would like.

Gaps

There are two specific reasons why you should just leave gaps in your writing, which you can come back and fill in later, for any information or words that you either don't know or don't remember.

First, if you follow the advice of CB#13, which states *"You shouldn't leave gaps and guesses in your writing,"* you will continually sever the essential connection with your AW each time you stop to research or ponder. As a result, nothing of any length or depth will ever be given the space and freedom that your AW desires. In the worst case scenario, of course, writer's block could surface, as well.

Second, a time and place during the beginning of the revision stage has been specifically reserved for you to go back through your entire manuscript and fill in all of the gaps you created. Waiting until then also allows you to do all the research that is necessary for your work, without wasting time, money, and energy through the collection of facts and information that you will probably never use through prewriting research.

Keep the Flow Going by Ending in the Middle and Warming Up Before Resuming

We are a people who desire an immediate sense of fulfillment and accomplishment. If we are dissatisfied with a movie or a sporting event, or a show on television, we immediately switch the channel.

In regards to reading, fulfilling that desire for a sense of accomplishment translates to reading through to the end of a chapter or a section in a book before stopping. However, when this same tactic is applied to our writing, it is completely counterproductive. For when we conclude a writing session at the end of a section or chapter, it makes it very difficult and sometimes impossible to reinvigorate the same energy and flow when attempting to reconnect with our own voice and style during the next writing session.

To make it easiest for yourself to reconnect with

"Put all your eggs in one basket and – WATCH THAT BASKET."
Mark Twain

"Do what you can, with what you have, with where you are."
Theodore Roosevelt

where you were, how you felt, and what you were saying, always conclude a writing session in the middle of a section or chapter. Then, all you will have to do the next day to reconnect with the flow from your previous writing session is to enter into your AW connected state and recopy the last few words which you wrote from your most previous session. The result will not only make it easy to maintain your essential flow and momentum from session to session, but will also offer your writing a necessary seamlessness between scenes, sections, and/or chapters.

While CB# 14, *"It is a bad idea to stop writing before you have completed a scene or section,"* is excellent advice for readers, it is poor advice for those of us who write what readers read.

"The very purpose of existence is to reconcile the glowing opinion we hold of ourselves with the appalling things that other people think about us.
Quentin Crisp

Just Let the Words Fly

So many of even the most respected authors are very weak in their understandings and use of the formalities of writing. Proving that, yes, grammar, syntax, and spelling are important, but completely secondary to the passion that can touch us all beyond all of our differences, and completely disproving CB# 15, which states, *"You have to be highly educated in spelling, grammar, and syntax to be a good writer."*

The key to both releasing and maintaining that essential passion, though, comes through our ability to remain in connection with our AW's, who releases its expression at a rate of between 1200-1800 words an hour. When writing, by all means, just allow the words to fly out of you, which will enable you to stay within the necessary range of speed, which will insure that you are remaining connected to your AW.

"You'll get no laurel crown for outrunning a burro."
Martial, 40-104 A.D.

Writing as Fast as You Can

While I was with the Pirates, we once had a young player who was a great athlete but far from being one of the brightest persons you could ever meet. Shortly after we had called him up from the minor

Tom Bird - ~~Write~~ Right From God

leagues and added him to our roster, he was installed as a mainstay at third base. Defensively, third base, since it is so close to home plate, is a reactionary position. The ball comes at you so fast off the bat of the hitter that either you immediately know what to do with it or you're maimed for life.

This young player had grown up in a baseball family. In fact, his father had been a famous big leaguer. So he was very familiar with the game, which helped him perform marvelously at his position as our third baseman.

However, it wasn't too long after he arrived, that the club decided to move him over to shortstop. Shortstop is commonly referred to as *"the thinking man's position,"* because from there a player can control the entire infield. It is also nearly twice the distance from home plate as third base. So a player stationed at shortstop is often given much more time to ponder his or her move or reaction to a play.

This one young player, as mentioned, was a phenomenal third baseman. However, he was a terrible defensive shortstop. After one game in which he had committed several errors, he was asked by a well-meaning reporter why it was that he was such a good third baseman, but yet was not nearly as competent at his new position of shortstop.

A brighter player would have taken the question as an insult, but not this young player, who responded immediately without any bias or negative reaction at all.

"Well ya know," he began in his broken New Jersey accent, *"when I was over at third base, you know, kinda like, when the ball was hit to me it got there real fast. But at shortstop, it bounces and bounces and bounces and takes a lot longer to get to me. In fact, it takes so long to get to me that I've got a lot of time to think about what it is that I am going to do with it when it finally gets there. And this always screws me up because every time I think, I screw up."*

"Every time I think, I get screwed up." How so true, not only in baseball and with so much in life, but how especially true with your writing, as well. Thinking, of course, is a byproduct of the critical/logi-

"If wisdom were offered me with the proviso that I should keep it shut up and refrain from declaring it, I should refuse. There's no delight in owning anything unshared."
Seneca, First Century, A.D.

"There are hazards in anything one does, but there are greater hazards in doing nothing."
Shirley Williams

170

cal mind. Feeling is a byproduct of your AW. Thus when writing effectively, it is in your best interest to always be feeling and not thinking.

The best way to avoid involving yourself with the latter is to write as fast as you can. For when you write as fast as you can, you will stay within that AW connected state and there will be no room for the unnecessary interruptions, interferences, and input that come through thinking.

"After a time, you may find that having is not so pleasing a thing, after all, as wanting. It is not logical, but it is often true."
Spock, "Star Trek"

As well, the slowness, confusion, and lack of confidence that comes with the string of unnecessary thought patterns and interruptions thrown up by the critical/logical mind can cause a book or screenplay at times to take several years to be completed. This situation causes another significant dilemma, for our emotions, understanding, interpretations, and reactions grow as human beings every day. In the course of a few years, our viewpoint on many a major situation will have changed and altered substantionally. These alterations in opinions and viewpoint will all be reflected in how your writing is eventually projected, leading to a massive inconsistency of voice and viewpoint in your work, which will terribly skew whatever message that it is which your AW is attempting to release through you.

Each book or screenplay represents one major idea, feeling, and/or expression. If the true meaning of what it is that you are writing is skewed because of your consistently altering viewpoint and voice, the essence of what it is that your AW is trying to release will be lost.

How fast is fast enough, though? As mentioned previously, my experience has shown me that the slowest speed at which the AW projects itself is approximately 1200 words per hour. The average speed is around 1500 words an hour. The highest consistent speed that I have ever seen sustained through an author is approximately 2200 words an hour. Remaining at as high of a speed as possible maintains your necessary connection with your AW, and ostracizes any and all forms of counterproductive intervention from your critical/logical mind.

To be able to release your AW at as high of a

speed as possible, it is first of all essential for you to see what your fastest writing speed is while in an AW connected state. So let's do that right now.

Your Maximum Present Writing Speed

For this exercise you will need either a digital watch or clock, or one with a second hand, a large piece of lineless writing paper and your pen.

Step 1. Follow your routine for relaxing and for getting into your AW connected state.

Step 2. Once there, envision, in great detail, your *"most recent significant loss."* Stay with this image, as you have done with all of those in the past, until you feel as if you are back there once again.

"To find themselves in the presence of true greatness many men find it necessary only to be alone."
Tom Masson

Step 3. After you have achieved the above state, open your eyes, note the time on your watch or clock, and then allow your feelings to pour out of you for exactly six minutes. If you choose to continue writing beyond that time, simply note where it was that you were, at that six minute mark, and continue writing.

Step 4. After you have finished writing, count the average number of words in an average looking line leading up to the six minute mark and write that number down. Then count the number of lines you wrote during those six minutes.

Step 5. To come up with your present maximum writing speed while in an AW connected state, multiply the two numbers. Then multiply your sum by ten. If you want to be extremely thorough, you can run this exercise a few different times and come up with an average for your trials. However, I have not found a substantial variance between the results of the first trial and the average of several.

How to Direct Your Maximum Speed With Your Writing

Now it's time to extend your maximum speed to the two hour segments you will be expected to write each day to complete the writing of your book or screenplay in record time. With all of the writing you have done up to this point, and because of all the once cumbersome barriers you have rid yourself of, not to mention the confidence you have picked up as the result of the directional exercises which you have participated in, the following should prove to be no more than a final tune up for you.

However, it is important that you continue to repeat the following until you can sustain your maximum writing speed over two consecutive hours. Then and only then will you be fully ready for the next chapter and your most exciting chore yet. Successfully directing your efforts on this exercise will pay mega dividends, as you will see. For this exercise, you will need to have a watch or a clock nearby.

> *"Wisdom enterth not into a malicious mind."*
> Rabelais

> *"An optimist may see a light where there is none. But must the pessimist always run to blow it out?*
> Michael De Saint-Pierre

Step 1. By now you should have a good understanding of how much space on your lineless, chosen writing surface you will cover over the course of one hour of writing. For example, if your maximum writing speed is 1600 words per hour, how many pieces of your chosen writing surface would that cover? If you're not quite sure, take some time now to figure that out. Then draw a solid, straight line across your surface where you would have to write to reach your maximum output for an hour.

After you have done that, then mark back from there where you would need to reach every fifteen minutes to achieve your ultimate one hour goal. Then beginning from where you left off for the maximum limit for your one hour goal, mark off on an additional writing surface(s) the same distance for your second hour of writing at your maximum speed.

Step 2. Take whatever steps that you need to reach your AW connected state.

Step 3. Clear your mind and allow something or someone who you have never met before to enter into your mind. Take a few moments to study the facial features, the eyes, posture, smell, disposition of this being and your own reaction to he or she or it. Then allow a second person, bird, fish, animal, or thing to enter into your mind. Ask them their names and then ask all who are present to answer the following four questions:

1) How did they meet?

2) What was it that drew them all together?

3) What is it that they are meant to do together?

4) Why?

As you have done with all of your other writing up to this point, allow your AW to paint a picture of their responses in your mind.

Step 4. Open your eyes, take note of the time, and allow the words of their story to pour out of you. Don't overreact to the fact that you are attempting to write at a certain pace. Relaxing and giving into the speed and inspiration of your AW is the key. So just relax and make sure to blow out any tension that you may be feeling.

Step 5. Write until the conclusion of your appointed two hours.

"Love thy neighbor as thyself, but choose your neighbor."
Louise Beal

Did you make your goal of maintaining your maximum writing speed over the two hours? If so, congratulations! If that is the case, you are ready to move on and commence the formal writing of your book or screenplay.

If you were unable to maintain your maximum speed over the two hours, don't worry. Simply modify the questions that you asked your characters and then repeat the exercise over again the next day, the next day, the next day, and the next day, if you need to, maintaining this exercise for a maximum of five consecutive days.

You are ready to move on to the next chapter if you either maintain your writing speed for two consecutive hours during any one of these exercises, or if you have performed the above task over five consecutive days.

Next comes the opportunity that you have worked so hard and waited so diligently to experience: the release of your book or screenplay. You are more than prepared, as I'm sure you already feel inside, for this experience.

"Every situation – nay, every moment – is of infinite worth; for it is the representative of a whole eternity."
Goethe

For by this time, you have knocked down all of the emotional, psychological, and logistical barriers that have stood in your way up to this time. You have a crystal clear vision, for the first time in your life and as the result of *The Living Outline*, of what it is that has been dying to get out of your for so long. Your attitude toward the possibilities of your success has substantially shifted toward the positive; you are now committed in the proper way. You have learned two ingenious writing techniques that are sure to generate your success; you're fully schooled in the use of both of them; everything that could have stood in your way has been removed and/or dealt with. You're writing better, deeper and faster than you ever could have imagined; your AW has been released – you're ready. Time to turn the page and live the literary experience of your life.

Oh yeah, as far as CB# 16, *"It takes forever to write a book or screenplay"* that is only true if you're inadequately prepared to approach it properly, and/or you don't know what you're doing; neither of which is the case with you.

"Working with Tom, Michael, and Carol moved me from a 'far-out-there' perspective on my book to a more realistic version. I started over, keeping only the title and one month later, had finished a more grounded and marketable first draft."
Jeannie Guthrie, Atlanta, GA

"Each year for the last six years "Start My Book" has appeared regularly on my list of goals and gone no farther. Now, thanks to Tom, three short weeks after the Intensive Writers' Retreat, it's FINISHED!! Wow!!"
Sue Christensen, Flagstaff, AZ

Chapter Fifteen:
Allowing Your AW to Write Your Project for You

CB# 17 states that *"Writers are responsible for creating books." Ahhhhhhhhh*! Is there any more of a frightening statement than that one? *"Authors create books,"* which means that you somehow have to be able to take credit for and recreate the brilliance you have seen come through your writing even if you have no idea where it came from in the first place.

Your critical/logical mind freaks out, *"There's no way that we can do that!"* Then it thinks for a moment. *"But we have to,"* it explains to itself, *"because we're in a bind, we said we were going to do this via that damned contract, so we have to. So the first thing we have to do is research, lots of it, maybe even years of it. Then we have to buff up on our grammar, punctuation, spelling, and..."*

The very thought of creation brings forth that sort of panic, and it should. Because frankly, you do not by

"The price of greatness is responsibility."
Winston Churchill

yourself have the ability to follow-through on the project you feel called to complete. Thank God for our AWs. For because of our AWs, all we have to do is leave the writing up to them. Any other approach other than that, of course, is completely counterproductive. And you have learned how to do everything that you need to do to best facilitate the release of this everyday miracle into your life.

Okay, let's go over your checklist to make sure that you will have everything that you need for this grand and glorious journey on which you are just about to embark:

> "One way to get high blood pressure is to go mountain climbing over molehills."
> Earl Wilson

1) *By now you should have purchased the desired number of pens and the necessary number of sheets of your chosen writing surface.*

2) *All of your contracts, especially the one meant to go to me, should have been sent out.*

3) *Your Living Outline should be posted and within clear view.*

4) *A weekly writing schedule of no less than two hours a day, six days a week should have been arranged.*

5) *Those in your life or with whom you share a home or office, or wherever it is that you write, should have been warned about the necessary private time that is needed for your writing, and warned that you will enforce your rights in this regard at all costs.*

Here are the components about your writing to keep in mind, as well, that will insure the successful completion of your project.

Read over the following list at least once every week, unless you run into a problem or a stoppage with your writing. In the case of the latter, immediately turn to this page, read over the following to see which of the suggestions, you have innocently forgotten or written in violation of. Then simply make whatever alterations are necessary in your approach to your writing and you will be healed.

> *"Capture the moment, whoever you are. None of us is here forever."*
> Adrain, 1958-1991

> *"For me a picture should be something likeable, joyous and pretty... yes, pretty. There are enough ugly things in life for us not to add them."*
> Pierre Auguste Renoir

1) *Always write as fast as you can. If for some reason your writing begins to lag or slow down, follow the drill posted in the last chapter on extending your writing speed. If you simply take a few minutes out of your writing time to focus on that, you will be right back up to your maximum speed and flow in no time.*

2) *Always precede any writing, or reading of your writing, by first following The Three R's of Writing.*

3) *"The cards" can be used not only for clearing as they were in Chapter Nine, but they can be used for problem solving, as well. So if you ever feel confused and lost with any aspect of your writing, all you have to do is to pull out some cards and just start brainstorming about how you feel. In no time at all your real problem will be brought to the surface, faced, understood, and taken care of so that you may continue on your way.*

4) *Do not edit, review, or read your work as you are writing. Save all of that until the final steps outlined in the next chapter.*

5) *Leave gaps for any bits of information or facts that a need may pop up for but which you don't have at your disposal at the present time. Remember, there is no need to panic. Panic automatically shuts down an AW connected state. All that needs to be researched will be covered in the activities outlined in the last step of the next chapter.*

6) *Take time to consistently reinforce each one of your successful writing outlines, no matter how large or small.*

7) *If any potentially distracting thoughts pop into your mind, dump them into your narrow right hand column and get back to your writing.*

8) *Work on your writing two hours a day, six days a week, no matter what happens. Don't judge your experience. Just stay within the lines of the*

program and all you ever wanted will pan out for you.

9) *Make sure to never conclude a writing session at the end of a chapter or section. Remember to warm back up at the beginning of each writing session by recopying the last 20-30 words that you wrote during your most previous session.*

10) *Remember to just let the words fly out of you and onto the boards, allowing your AW to take you and your writing wherever it is that you are both destined to go.*

11) *Outside of required reading for your job or profession, and magazines and newspapers, don't do any reading for the next few weeks during which time you will be completing your book or screenplay. After you have found your voice, you can go back to reading whatever it is that you want.*

> "Unprovided with original learning, unformed in the habits of thinking, unskilled in the arts of compositions, I resolved to write a book."
> Edward Gibbon

A Few Last Minute Reminders

When beginning the writing of your project, please keep in mind:

- *The writing of any major project usually starts off slowly. Until you both get used to each other, don't allow any early sluggishness to rattle you. Just stay within the routine and in no time your book or screenplay will have adjusted to you and you to it. When that happens, you both will begin operating as one and all will go a lot smoother.*

- *No matter how much preparatory work we have done up to this point, you will still not know exactly where it is that you are going with your writing from day-to-day. Remember, this is your AW's way of keeping you interested.*

- *Your project will end all on its own. You will*

> "People who live in glass houses have to answer the bell."
> Bruce Patterson

also be given very little advance notice of when this will happen. About forty-five minutes before it concludes is usually the norm. The reason for this short notice is so that your critical mind will not have time to come out and screw up your execution.

- Remember that all you need to know you, already know and all you need to have, you already have in your possession. To remind yourself of this fact, all you have to do is to look back through this book and all that you have already accomplished at any time which you choose.

Let's Go!

Okay, it's time to begin. I will get you started, but from this point forward it will be you and your AW writing your project. Of course, I will always be standing in the near background, smiling fondly.

Step 1. Get into your AW connected state.

Step 2. Pull out a piece of your chosen writing surface, and in the center of it, write either the name of your lead character, if you are writing fiction, or a word or two that best captures the theme or the topic of your work if you are writing non-fiction.

Step 3. Allow yourself to completely free associate any thoughts or feelings, whether they are directly tied to that which you will be writing or not, by releasing them onto the lineless piece of paper before you.

Step 4. Once anything longer than a prepositional phrase on your character or theme pops out, immediately transfer your efforts to a second piece of paper and allow your project to begin writing itself.

No matter how many days or weeks it takes, do

"The world is moving so fast these days that the man who says it can't be done is generally interrupted by someone doing it."
Henry Emerson Fosdick

"You can convert your style into riches."
Quentin Crisp

not proceed onto the next chapter until your project has written itself. Go!

Chapter Sixteen: Enhancing

"On with the dance, let the joy be unconfined!" Is my motto, whether there's any dance to dance or any joy to unconfine."
Mark Twain

CB# 18 states that, "*To be a successful writer, you need to edit and edit and edit your work over and over and over again*". That is only true if you have not taken the necessary and proper steps to insure consistent contact with your AW, so as to provide the necessary depth and direction essential to the success of whatever it is that you will write. If you have done that, though, then editing becomes a completely counterproductive, destructive drill engineered and contracted by your critical/logical mind for the sole, selfish purpose of demolishing the essence and beauty of what you and your AW have created.

As previously mentioned, fear of success is the primary cause for this sort of reaction. It is because of this typical dysfunctional reaction that I have chosen to instead employ the use of the word "enhance" to differentiate between what it is that normally happens and what it is that we will be doing together. For by no

183

means will we be seeking to destroy your work in any shape or form. To the contrary, our sole purpose will be to take something that already has all of the necessary ingredients and which is good, and just make it better.

The First Sweep Through

*Ricky Ricardo: There you go again, wanting something that you haven't got.
Lucy Ricardo: I do not, I just want to see what I haven't got that I don't want.
I Love Lucy*

Remember that it is essential that you be in an AW connected state not only when you write, but when you read over, revise, or enhance whatever it is that you have written. Keep that in mind as you begin the following exercise, which will take several sessions to complete. From this point forward, just stay with the same writing schedule which you have utilized to complete the rough draft of your project. However, instead of writing your work during that time, devote your time to enhancing, and in no time at all your project will be fully revised, polished, and complete.

Repeat the following steps each day until you have completely read through your manuscript and have noted any and all major changes you feel your work needs.

Step 1. Enter into your AW connected state.

Step 2. Read through your book or screenplay, noting any and all major changes or alterations you would like to make to your work.

> Major changes are defined as any alterations or rearrangements or additions that directly affect the general theme or direction of what you have already written. This does not include grammatical changes and/or the correction of typographical mistakes. The easy way that I have found to note your changes in this regard is to just write down any suggestions you may have on "post 'em" notes and then to place the notes on your chosen writing surface wherever it is that you are suggesting for your changes to be made.

Step 3. Do not move on to the next step until you have fully completed this one.

> "Life is like an overlong drama through which we sit being nagged by the vague memories of having read the reviews."
> John Updike

After You Have Completed the Above

Step 1. Enter into your AW connected state.

Step 2. Make whatever general changes that you have proposed for your book or screenplay. You may have to, of course, use several other pieces of your chosen writing surface to do so. It may take several days to complete this task, if not weeks. In that case, simply follow these two steps each time you go into your manuscript to make the necessary changes, rearrangements, or additions. Don't move onto the next step until you are fully completed with this one.

Post Writing Research

After you have completed the making of any and all necessary, general changes to your project, it is time to convert your daily writing time to the use of two other activities.

First of all, it is essential to insure that you are in your AW connected state before you look back through your project in this or any other phase like it. Taking time to relax is good, but it is often not enough if you aren't writing on a consistent basis.

> "All through the five acts he played King as though under the momentary apprehension that someone else was about to play the Ace."
> Eugene Field

So, beginning now, it is essential that you begin devoting one third of your allotted writing time each day to more work with "the cards". Do not devote any more than one third of your allotted time to writing in this fashion. Otherwise, you will become so obsessed with whatever it is that is coming out that you may neglect your other responsibilities.

As I am sure you are beginning to sense already,

there is a very gentle and necessary balance that exists between the expression of new material and the revision of what you have written already. You have gotten used to, maybe even become positively addicted to, the connected release of your AW. You now need it as it feeds you. This is where the positively addictive aspects of writing which I spoke about earlier come into play. This connection not only feeds your life but the entire writing experience and whatever goes along with it including your post writing research. So make sure that you fully and consistently devote one third of your time each day to the completion of your next project.

What will come out at this time will most possibly be the beginning of your *Living Outline* for your next project. Your feelings in this regard probably fall to one extreme or another. You may have felt that you had several works vying for your time and attention when you first started with this program, only to discover that one idea was trying desperately to get your attention in a wide variety of ways.

For your AW, whom doesn't want to confuse you and thus cause you unnecessary pain or discomfort, would not initially offer you more than one idea at a time until you had the opportunity to become familiar with writing a work of that length. Or on the other hand, you may have initially had a challenging time believing that you even had one book or screenplay inside of you. Then when this second idea comes streaming through you are totally and absolutely aghast.

"Resolve to know thyself: and know, that he who finds himself, loses his misery."
Matthew Arnold

Either way, you will be amazed at what comes out and with the ease and speed by which it is released. Get used to it. Your life has been and will continue to get more and more exciting. All that you will learn through your connection with your AW will lead you to deeper conclusions and understandings about the other areas of your life. These understandings will enable you to become a beacon of what is possible for all of us. if you are just willing to reach outside of yourself for the unconditional love, acceptance and assistance that awaits us all.

Make sure to keep that connection flowing free

with your use of "the cards" each day during this phase, and then once you have filled in all of the gaps you had left in your book or screenplay, move onto the next step.

The Colors of the Rainbow

No one will ever know the purpose and meaning of your writing, what and how you are attempting to express through it, better than you, which is why it is best for both you and your work if you stay intimately connected with it through the revisionary stages.

In this step, you will fine tune your words with the precision that a grand piano is tuned. For this drill, you will need one pack of four different colored highlighters. Since this step is one of a very conscious nature, it is essential that you continue to devote one third of your writing time to your use of "the cards".

If your work with "the cards" has taken you to the point where you can construct your *Living Outline* on your bulletin board, go ahead and do it. You will probably have noticed already that your work with "the cards" led you almost directly to the flushing out of your archetypes before moving quickly onto the outlining of your next work, without touching on the cathartic stage much at all. This is normal for this stage of your development, since the vast majority, if not all, of your necessary cathartic clearing took place during your first interchange with "the cards". If you have already moved past or do venture past the confines of your *Living Outline* during these steps, simply follow the exact same steps with your new project, that you followed with your fist, and let'er rip.

In regard to your highlighters, we will be restricting their use to the making of initially three separate sweeps through your project. On the first pass through, designate one highlighter for the making of all of your *action verbs*. On the second sweep through, take another marker and highlight all of your *passive verbs*. On the third pass through, use the last two markers to highlight all of your *adjectives* and *adverbs*.

"The last quarter of a century of my life has been pretty constantly and faithfully devoted to the study of the human race - that is to say, the study of myself, for in the individual person I am the entire human race compacted together. I have found that there is no ingredient of the race which I do not possess in either a small way or a large way."
Mark Twain

"I never think of the future. It comes soon enough."
Albert Einstein

These three sweeps through your manuscript may take days if not weeks, as will the following steps. If you are confused and unsure on these different forms of language, this is a good time to go back and brush up on your grammar.

Once you have completed your highlighting, go through your manuscript and first focus solely on each of your action verbs. With each and every action verb, ask yourself if you are using the most appropriate and expressive verb possible in each and every case. If you have not done so, change whatever you have written to the appropriate verb.

After you have completed your sweep of the action verbs, then focus solely and completely upon your passive verbs. The liability with passive verbs is that they carry absolutely no imagery, and without that ability to make your reader feel, hear, see, smell, or taste something, you will lose connection with him or her.

Too many passive verbs, especially following consecutively in a row, will bore your reader or even possibly put him or her to sleep. Of course, you don't want to do that. So when focusing upon your passive verbs, ask yourself, in each and every case, if there is a way you could possibly alter your sentences and/or paragraphs to rid your manuscript of so many passive verbs, and supplement in their place action verbs.

Verbs are the pulse of each one of your sentences. They are responsible for, direct, and project forward the most imagery. When they are perfectly attuned not only will your words sing, but a substantial portion of your adjectives and adverbs will have become obsolete, as well.

"If you want to win anything-a race, yourself, your life – you have to go a little berserk."
George Sheehan

You now need to make one final pass through to pluck out any adjectives and adverbs that are no longer needed, whose presence, if left untouched, may lead to your project being seen as "wordy."

Once you have completed this step, which is designed to not only fine tune your manuscript, but to re-educate your AW to write even better and more effectively from this point forward, you are free to go onto the next phase.

The Pianist in Us All

This step signals the typing of your manuscript into your computer. For this, you will need an easel or some sort of structure that will enable a few of your chosen writing surfaces to be held at eye level, so you may comfortably type your book or screenplay into your computer. There are a few responsibilities to keep in mind when performing this step.

First, continue to devote one third of your designated writing time to working with your next project.

Second, make sure that you are in as relaxed of a state as possible when you are typing. If you want to sip on some type of relaxing beverage or play some relaxing music, now is the time to do so.

Being as relaxed as possible is essential to insure that you are as sensitive as possible to the flow of your material, which will have been significantly altered with all of the changes you will have made. By being as relaxed as possible, your heightened sensitivity will enable you to first sense and then smooth out any and all disjointed aspects of your text, which will have been caused by rearranging, adding, subtracting, or making general adjustments to your material.

When doing this myself, I envision myself as a concert pianist who becomes at one with the music which is playing through me. In that way, I can feel the rhythm of my writing and make any necessary alterations to it as I allow my books to flow through my fingers and into the computer.

When you have finished entering your manuscript into your computer, go onto the next step.

Let Your Computer Go to Work for You

Now is the time to let your computer go to work for you. Once your manuscript has been typed into your computer, run it through your spell check and correct any misspellings.

I am not an advocate of computerized grammar checkers. I just don't believe in allowing anyone else's unknowing and/or uncaring opinion to influence how I

"I am earnest; I will not equivocate; I will not excuse; I will not retreat a single inch; I will be heard."
William Lloyd Garrison

feel it best to communicate. You may feel differently. If so, run your manuscript through your grammar checker, as well.

Once you have run it through your spell check and possibly through your grammar checker, print out a hard copy of your manuscript.

One Final Read Through

"Watch out for emergencies. They are your big chance!"
Fritz Reiner

You should be continuing to work with your newest project as you enter this final phase in completion of your initial project. If you have fallen off on your commitment to your second work for whatever reason, get back to it. You should still be devoting a minimum of one third of your allotted writing time to it each day.

During this final phase of what will have been a very exciting ride, you will find yourself feeling ambivalent. One part of you will be wildly excited to get this project completed. While the other side of you will be feeling sad. This is normal. For what you have written is to you like your literary child, who is just about to fly from the nest. There is a part of you that is anxious for your child to leave. While there is another portion who is terribly sad to have to say good-bye, and to have to let go of all that you two have shared.

It is important to keep in mind as you read over your manuscript one last time to insure that you check for any necessary, flow based adjustments, which may have resulted from all the changes that you may have made to your rough draft.

"After a time, you may find that having is not so pleasing a thing, after all, as wanting. It is not logical, but it is often true." Spock – Star Trek

It is also essential during this parting to keep in mind that this child you have released will be with you always. No matter where the two of you choose to venture from this point forward, the connection, love, and interchange that has been shared will always be with you.

Finish reading through your manuscript one final time and then move onto the next step.

Publication

A writer's success is often determined by his or her success with getting their material published, with which I totally disagree. Even though my *How To Get Published* course has been the cornerstone of my teaching for the last two decades, I do not believe that you have to publish to be successful. I believe that the most valuable benefits from writing come as the result of the experience itself. The joy, understanding, acceptance, and wisdom that come to you through connecting with your AW is unparallel by any financial wealth or notoriety that could possibly come to you through publication.

"I cannot give you the formula for success, but I can give you the formula for failure – which is: Try to please everybody."
Herbert Bayard Swope

However, if publication is something that your heart is calling you to do, then by all means pursue it. For the essence of writing is sharing. First your AW shares with you as you share your trust with it. A manuscript manifests as a result. If you feel so called, you can share that work with others through publication. If that be the case, I recommend my book entitled *How To Get Published*, which takes the same humanistic and highly effective approach to this task, as well.

If you do not feel called to do so, then whatever it is that you have written was meant for you and you alone.

"Do what you can, with what you have, with where you are."
Theodore Roosevelt

Either way though, you will have succeeded in doing what so many aspire to do, yet so few accomplish. Congratulations, you are a very special person. However, for those of you who may wish to publish for whatever reason, I felt you may enjoy the following recollection from one of my students.

Testimonial

Rosemary O'Keeffe on the submission of her query letter

"I had a story I wanted to tell. No wait. I should rephrase that. I had a story I wanted to tell and get published. Big Difference.

"I keep the telephone of my mind open to peace, harmony, health, love and abundance. Then, whenever doubt, anxiety or fear try to call me, they keep getting a busy signal – and soon they'll forget my number."
Edith Armstrong

"The challenge came not so much in the wanting or the actual writing. For me the real challenge rose up to greet me in the form of a query letter

"At first I thought of it as a epic smashed onto one page. Impossible, And as long as I kept that image, it remained impossible.

"After a few sorry attempts, I decided to try a different approach. If advertisers could condense a two hour movie into a one minute montage for television publicity, then I should be able to do the same with my book. And it worked.

"It took a few more efforts to get it right, but when I finally hit my stride, it flowed readily. I liked what I had written; however, was it good enough to influence the literary agents?

"Mass production started in my office as over 200 of the queries slid from the laser printer. Hot after them came my cover letter. I kept that simple and to the point. This correspondence was destined for the desks of busy people. They did not have the time to weed through the philosophical reasons behind my wanting to write this story.

"I have to confess my hands shook while I stuffed the first few envelopes. That quickly dissipated and the task turned into a chore. This was definitely the boring part of writing.

"On the way to the post office. I glanced at the box in the passenger's seat. There it sat, a cardboard container cradling my first real endeavor at writing in earnest. I shoved stacks into the mailbox, sending each bundle on its way with a special invocation. Then I drove home and waited.

"At times the wait dragged on endlessly. On the day the first few envelopes turned up in our mailbox, the wait suddenly seemed all too short. How could these people have seriously considered my story in such a short time? Well what did they know anyway?

"One thing I had done while I waited, besides write, was to train and prepare myself for the rejections that would surely come. I forced myself to realize my story could not possibly satisfy everyone, just as no book appeals to the masses completely.

"I also reminded myself a rejection from an agent

was not done on a personal level. The person in New York or Georgia or California did not know me, they only knew my story. And they either liked it or they didn't.

"So, by the time the first replies arrived, I had prepared myself to face them as professionally as possible. I knew to do otherwise would mean the end of my writing.

"Overall, sending out my first query left me both elated yet slightly fearful. Like a bashful suitor, I had laid my emotions on the line and waited to see if they would end up smashed to bits.

"Waiting for the outcome could be compared to bungee jumping. You sink like a rock to the end of the cord, then rebound up - almost, but not quite - to where you started. Finally you dangle near the ground, reading each and every reply. Interestingly enough, the rush that comes with the challenge of the jump is enough to make most writers want to do it again – and again – and again.

"Surrounded by mountains of paper, lists, stamps, and envelopes as I prepared to send out an initial query to a good number of literary agents, I felt like a piece of taffy being dragged in two completely different directions. One minute I was excited and optimistic: 'One of these agents is bound to think that this is a good idea for a book and will want to represent me. I know what I want to say in this book and I think I can help people even if only so that they won't think they're quite as crazy as I was when I entered midlife. I've wanted to be a writer since I was twelve years old. It's time to get started.'

"In the very next second, doubt and the black edge of that wonderfully resilient inner 'spoiler,' that big ol' abusive critic from the darkest corner of the underworld, reared its ugly mug and, breathing fire, whispered, 'No one wants another book on midlife. Doesn't Gail Sheehy have that territory pretty well covered anyway? Besides, who ever told you that you could be a writer? You are wasting your time and energy here. And you've spent over fifty dollars on stamps, you jerk.'

"In the midst of this raging inner conflict I contin-

"The successful people are the ones who can think up things for the rest of the world to keep busy at." Don Marquis

"In no other period of history were the learned so mistrustful of the divine possibilities in man as they are now." Gopi Krishna

ued to lick, stamp, stuff, and mail. Though I did notice that a few of the envelope edges were singed as I dropped them into the postal box."

Where to Go Now

> *"It is the chiefest point of happiness that a man is willing to be what he is."*
> *Desiderius Erasmus, 1465-1536*

As it was with your concluding of your manuscript, this is an ambivalent time for me, as well. I am happy and proud beyond belief that we have come this far on this journey together. For that, I will always be eternally grateful. But I am also a bit sad. Saying *"good bye"* has never been one of my stronger attributes. So instead I will just visualize us continuing to work together in some manner or form. For I choose to see the independence you have acquired not as a *"good bye,"* but instead as a *"hello,"* a *"hello"* to the real you that I was offered the distinct privilege to be a part in birthing.

Thank you from the bottom of my heart for that. Thank you, as well, for all that you will do with your AW and your *"new you"* from this point forward.

Always be yourself. For being anything less will not only be doing you a great disservice, but, most of all, the world and all that makes it up would suffer greatly. We need you. So I choose to part by just saying *"hello","welcome"*, and *"we're all so glad you're here"*.

BOOKS AND PROGRAMS OFFERED BY TOM BIRD

TOM BIRD'S 2002 SELECTIVE GUIDE TO LITERARY AGENTS – The ultimate consumer's guide for the aspiring author looking to land the right literary agent. Newly updated, this year's edition boasts of nearly 400 of the industry's top literary agents. Over the last seventeen years, this guide has led thousands to the acceptances they deserve. A must for anyone who wants to sell screenplays or books of any type. Price $37.00.

TOM BIRD'S 2002 SELECTIVE GUIDE TO LITERARY AGENTS DISK – The same exact information as available in the book above, with the exception that this version is organized as a database on disk. This unique version allows you to access your chosen sources with a click of your mouse and to merge them all together, saving you days of precious time when submitting query letters. Price $89.00.

GETTING PUBLISHED NOW! – Recently revised and updated, this mainstay of Tom's teaching offers you absolutely everything that you will need to see your work in print, no matter what it is that you want to write. *How To Get Published* starts out with helping you decide upon and understand exactly what it is that you truly want to write, then takes you through the three steps that you need to see your work in print. Plenty of winning examples enclosed, including query letters and submission packages. If seeing your work in print is something that you have chosen to experience, this book presents opportunities never before available to you, and changes your life as a result. Price $36.00.

2002 Selective Guide to Literary Agents $37.00 $_____
2002 Selective Guide to Literary Agents Mail Merge $89.00 $_____
Getting Published Now! $36.00 $_____
(S&H $4.00 for 1-2 books, $6.00 for 3 or more)
Total Amount Due $_____

Ordering Information: Please make your checks out to: Tom Bird Seminars, Inc. and mail to, P. O. Box 4306, Sedona, AZ 86336. Or, fax Visa, MC, Discover, or AMX credit card information to 928/203-0264. Online Ordering is also available through Paypal via www.sojourninc.com. (Prices subject to change without notice.)

For further information, feel free to either give us a call at 928/203-0265 or visit out website at http://www.ambassu.com